GW00750188

Junkers Ju 188

Helmut Erfurth

MIDLAND
An imprint of
Ian Allan Publishing

Junkers Ju 188
© Bernard & Graefe Verlag, 2002, 2003

ISBN 1 85780 172 5

First published 2002 in Germany by
Bernard & Graefe Verlag, Bonn

Translation from original German text
by Ted Oliver

English language edition published 2003 by
Midland Publishing
4 Watling Drive, Hinckley, LE10 3EY, England
Tel: 01455 254 490   Fax: 01455 254 495
E-mail: midlandbooks@compuserve.com

Midland Publishing is an imprint of
Ian Allan Publishing Ltd

Worldwide distribution (except North America):
Midland Counties Publications
4 Watling Drive, Hinckley, LE10 3EY, England
Telephone: 01455 254 450   Fax: 01455 233 737
E-mail: midlandbooks@compuserve.com
www.midlandcountiessuperstore.com

North American trade distribution:
Specialty Press Publishers & Wholesalers Inc.
39966 Grand Avenue, North Branch, MN 55056
Tel: 651 277 1400   Fax: 651 277 1203
Toll free telephone: 800 895 4585
www.specialtypress.com

Design concept and layout
© 2003 Midland Publishing and
Stephen Thompson Associates

Printed in England by
Ian Allan Printing Ltd
Riverdene Business Park, Molesey Road,
Hersham, Surrey, KT12 4RG

Front cover illustration:
A Ju 188 on Bernburg Airfield.

Title page illustration:
**The Ju 188 V1, NF+KQ, became the official
first prototype of the Ju 188 series and was
converted and redesignated from the Ju 88 V44.**

Contents

Photo Credits

EADS Archive, Ottobrunn	15
IG Luftfahrtgeschichte (Aviation History) Archive, Sachsen-Anhalt, Halle	1
Photo-collection Regnat, Munich	5
Thomas Erfurth, Dessau	6
Martin Kuras, Dessau	1
Author's collection	50
Bernard & Graefe Archive	1

Preface

The Ju 188 originated from the Junkers Flugzeug- und Motorenwerke (Junkers Aircraft & Engine Works) in Dessau and was among the most well-known combat aircraft of World War Two. It was developed from 1941 out of the Ju 88B-series model as an interim solution until the Ju 288 was ready for operational use. Like no other combat aircraft, the Ju 188 incorporated the sum of all the military and tactical experience of frontline pilots as well as the most up-to-date technological design in aircraft construction and armament at that time in Germany.

Technical and scientific know-how and the knowledge derived from direct operational experience, together with the manpower potential of German industry, made it possible to create a combat aircraft in the shortest possible time. It was to serve as a symbol of technocracy in the Third Reich and play a significant role in the implementation of its radical political aims.

Although the Ju 188 did not count among the most prolific aircraft in terms of volume (1,237 examples were built), it nevertheless represented an important segment of the largest German aircraft procurement programme: the Ju 88 'family' of aircraft. Seen as a whole, the programme from the Ju 88 to the Ju 488 represents a superb technological design and logistical concept – an almost unique example in the history of German aircraft manufacture.

Featuring a new type of smoothly contoured spherical full-view crew compartment, which greatly expanded the field of vision, the aircraft had enlarged wings and a similarly modified empennage, improved flying characteristics and two more powerful engines. These all contributed to the quality of its fighting capabilities. At the same time, continual modifications to the equipment and armament enabled a whole series of variants to be developed. These were

ideally configured to the particular role it was to fulfil and resulted in its operational employment as a fast level- and dive-bomber, and for special tasks, as a long-range reconnaissance and torpedo-carrier. It was also projected and built in prototype form as a high-altitude bomber and night-fighter, but these were not fully realised until the introduction of the Ju 388 programme. First and foremost, however, the Ju 188 served as an instrument of policy, the declared aim of which was the expansion of National Socialism in Europe that was to be implemented with the full power of the German military.

The 'face' of a Junkers Ju 188. It shows the characteristic features of a modern purpose-built aerodynamic and transparent cockpit canopy that offered its crew optimal vision and technically perfect operating conditions.

Chapter One

Delays

A Re-evaluation of Priorities

As a result of the experience gained by the flying formations in World War One, several military experts had already speculated on the subject of the strategic importance and the military and tactical role of a contemporary and future modern air force. Among them, Sir Hugh Trenchard, Commander-in-Chief of the Royal Air Force, and the US General Billy Mitchell, developed theories concerning the conduct of strategic air warfare. When opposing countries confronted each other in a military conflict, strategically concentrated air raids with heavy bombers had to so weaken the opponents' centres of industrial production that a rapid end to hostilities could be brought about.

Such considerations and war planning games were also conducted in France and Germany. Walter Wever was the first Chief of the General Staff of the newly established Luftwaffe from 1935 until his untimely death in 1936. He pursued this goal to develop strategic bombers and have them built in large numbers so as to be able in a future conflict to destroy, both operationally and tactically, the most strategically important industrial and military installations and transport routes in the heart of enemy territory. In his view, only by such means could swift military decisions be taken in the interests of conducting a successful offensive military and tactical operation.

This, however, represented a doctrine that was not supported by all military planners in the Luftwaffe (German Air Force) and the Wehrmacht (Armed Forces). After Wever's death, another direction was pursued in which the Luftwaffe was primarily to provide successful support to the Heer (Army), and it was mainly this strategic concept that was adopted by Reichsluftfahrtminister (Minister of Aviation) Hermann Göring and Generalluftzeugmeister (Chief of Air Procurement & Supply) Ernst Udet.

On the very day that Adolf Hitler came to power as Reichs Chancellor, 30th January 1933, the Office of Reichs Commissioner for Aviation was established in Berlin, which gave Hermann Göring the power to create a new Luftwaffe. As a pilot and former commanding officer of a Jagdgeschwader (Fighter Wing) in World War One, Hermann Göring had first-hand operational experience, but he also possessed a military-theoretical mentality as well as an organisational talent combined with considerable self-assurance.

Between 30th January and 12th February 1933, Hermann Göring initiated the first steps against the scientist and aircraft manufacturer Professor Hugo Junkers with the aim of appropriating not only the most modern research and production centres in Germany but also the several hundred patents encompassing aviation technology and logistics in order to build up a modern air arm. Appointed by Göring, State Secretary Erhard Milch thus set out to achieve what the supporters of the Reichswehr (German Army & Navy), representatives of the right wing of the government, and the commercial and industrial hierarchy had already begun at the end of the Weimar Republic: namely, the immediate hand-over by Hugo Junkers of all patent rights, failing which he would be charged with treason. Simultaneously, the Reich sought to block payment for all articles already delivered by him and to delete the Junkerswerke from the list of those enterprises that were to receive financial support within the framework of the Employment Procurement Programme. Placed under considerable psychological and physical pressure, several of his leading employees and family members having meanwhile been taken into protective custody, Junkers was forced to sign over the required Patent Transfer Agreement on 2nd June 1933. The scientific and technical way was thus paved for what was known as the ABC Programme – the creation of a modern Luftwaffe.

But even this did not satisfy Hermann Göring who had meanwhile been nominated Minister of Aviation on 5th May 1933. In accordance with a decision taken on 3rd October 1933 by the newly established RLM or Reichsluftfahrtministerium (German Air Ministry), Hugo Junkers was to hand over his majority holding of the company shares to a government-appointed executor. This occurrence, unique in the economic history and administration of justice in Germany, of a state-instituted coercion against the owner of one of the most significant enterprises, was primarily intended to achieve the appropriation of the scientific, technical and organisational know-how of Hugo Junkers and remove him from his own firm, particularly from aircraft and aero-engine manufacture. In the ensuing period of political and legal repression, during which he was forbidden from entering his firm's premises and placed under house arrest, Hugo Junkers was unable to withstand these coercive actions. He died on 3rd February 1935.

With the appointment of former Flick director Heinrich Koppenberg as Chairman of the Board of Directors of Junkers on 6th December 1933, the emphasis was shifted in the direction of rearmament. At this time, the re-equipment programme was already under way. In the initial phase, 400 examples of the Ju 52/3m to be used as auxiliary bombers were to be manufactured and delivered to the RLM up until 1935. Large-scale manufacturing contracts were also placed with the Flick ATG in Leipzig, and Blohm und Voss in Hamburg, which were quickly able to enter the field of air armament through the state-sanctioned use of Junkers' know-how. At the same time, several RLM specifications were issued to German aircraft firms to tender for suitable fighter aircraft and for light and medium bombers to be developed. Planning for heavy, so-called strategic bombers also formed a part of the air armament programme into 1936.

Adolf Hitler wanted the most modern and most powerful air force in the world within the shortest possible time. As part of the measures for shrugging off the armament limitations imposed by the Treaty of Versailles in 1919 and the re-introduction of general conscription in Germany, Hermann Göring announced the official implementation of the air armament programme as of 16th March 1935. Aircraft manufacturing centres and associated component delivery firms were quickly established almost everywhere in Germany. Since the Army and Navy weapons branches were also a part of this rearmament plan in which priorities had not been clearly defined beforehand, these developments naturally led to bottlenecks in the economy. On top of that were the war preparations and construction plans of the Organisation Todt from which all branches of weapons producers, including the armaments industry, would be able to profit, but which also needed additional capacity in terms of manpower and materials in no small measure.

Photograph on the opposite page:
An aerial view of JFM Dessau taken in 1938.

5

In order to establish rules that were binding on all parties, a programme was created for the increased production and refinement of raw materials, as well as the development of substitute materials, with the aim of using these as effectively as possible for the re-armament process. Particular emphasis was placed on the processing of iron ore and light metals, especially aluminium and magnesium alloys for the aviation industry. The production of mineral oils, synthetic rubber, artificial textile fibres and materials was also given priority status. Simultaneously, the largest possible raw materials and nutrition base was to be created so that in the event of war, particular shortfalls in materials and foodstuffs could be balanced out for a certain period of time before supplies from occupied countries became available.

This programme, announced at the NSDAP (National Socialist German Workers Party) Conference on 9th September 1936 in the shape of a second Four-Year Plan, was the responsibility of Hermann Göring. A self-sufficient independent organisation created especially for this purpose in 1938 and subordinate to the reorganised Reich Ministry of Economics co-ordinated the prescribed tasks with the respective branches of industry, individual

Reich ministries and the Army Co-ordination Office. From September 1943, the RfRuK or Reichsministerium für Rüstung und Kriegsproduktion (Reich Ministry for Armament and War Production) assumed this task, headed by Albert Speer. For Göring, the leadership of this organisation during the phase until 1938 meant a widening of his powers of authority which he exercised in the interest of his RLM. His main consideration, however, lay in the rapid build-up and expansion of the Luftwaffe. He thus concentrated on the manufacture of fighters and light bombers, so that questions concerning the tactical radius of penetration and increase in bombload played only a secondary role in his strategic planning.

As with other military planners on the General Staff, Hermann Göring allowed himself to be convinced that Germany need only employ all available resources for a short-term war, instead of having to consider emplacements over a lengthy period or for a multifront conflict. This confirmed the so-called 'Blitzkrieg' (Lightning War) strategy that during the initial phases of World War Two was undertaken with visible success by the Wehrmacht between 1939 and 1940. For this type of locally confined war, the Luftwaffe was able to fulfil its task of supporting troop movements effectively

through tactical air operations. Strategic long-range bombers were not envisaged in this concept of military planning and were therefore considered superfluous.

On 3rd June 1936, the Luftwaffe Chief of the General Staff, Walter Wever, an experienced pilot, took off together with the mechanic Krass in the RLM Squadron's Heinkel He 70 (D-UZON). It crashed immediately after lift-off from the airfield at Dresden, killing Wever. With his death, the RLM and the Wehrmacht lost their most persistent advocate of the necessity of operating multi-engined bombers deep in the heart of enemy territory.

Immediately following this tragic accident, Hermann Göring called a halt to further development of the two experimental strategic long-range bombers, the Dornier Do 19 and Junkers Ju 89, and concentrated large-scale production on medium bomber types such as the Do 17 and Heinkel He 111, of which test prototypes or pre-production examples already existed. Single-or twin-engined aircraft were much quicker to produce and more economic than four-engined bombers that required far more materials, additional specialist personnel engaged in manufacture of the aircraft and an increased need for trained pilots and maintenance crews.

A decisive factor in pursuing the 'Blitzkrieg' strategy in the German General Staff were the events in the Spanish Civil War in which the Luftwaffe with its newly developed dive-bombers and light bombers was able to test its aircraft under wartime conditions. This tactical use – the 'baptism of fire' – as Reichs Propaganda Minister Josef Goebbels termed it in his diaries kept during this conflict, convinced the last doubters of the correctness of this strategy. With the opening of hostilities against Poland on 1st September 1939, the world witnessed a demonstration of German 'Blitzkrieg' strategy that was so constituted, by means of barrages of fire attacks by the Luftwaffe and the rapid advance of ground troops, that capitulation was almost immediate. Equally decisive besides the rapid establishment of air superiority was the close liaison between the Luftwaffe and the ground forces with their tank formations.

The war against Denmark and Norway from 9th April 1940 also took the form of a 'Blitzkrieg', not only in the collaboration of the individual armed services but also in terms of the time involved. During the Norwegian Campaign, however, development failures soon became apparent, particularly with regard to covering the large transportation distances. Here, the first problems were encountered through the lack of long-range bombers or of bomber and fighter aircraft with a high depth of penetration. The attachment of auxiliary fuel tanks to extend the range resulted in a reduced bombload and a decrease in maximum speed that was particularly noticeable in tactical air combat.

During the Western Campaign, which began with the surprise attack on the Netherlands, an air armada supported the ground troops in their attacks. Within four days, the Allied formations of England and France lost their air power on the Continent, the Luftwaffe and ground formations having demonstrated their fighting strength in 'Blitzkrieg' operations.

Following the signing of the French capitulation on 22nd June 1940, the air war became concentrated on England. Now, although the German Navy entered the picture, it was primarily the Luftwaffe that was challenged. After initial Luftwaffe successes, the air battles over England turned out to be a fiasco. One by one, the misjudgements of the experts and military planners came to light. They had relinquished the long-range bomber and had consistently blocked a series of advanced projects and flight trials with new extended-range bombers and fighters. Added to that was the continued insistence on modifications and corrections to delivery schedules set by the RLM, which appeared acceptable on tactical or economic grounds but when viewed from the material, technical and organisational aspects caused even greater problems. The most important materials, and in aircraft manufacture that meant the most diverse light metal alloys, types of steel and materials such as Plexiglas, were rationed by the RLM or the Reich Economics Ministry, and were allocated different levels of priority in accordance with the various military and political considerations.

This was the position when the JFM AG in Dessau, following an internal company evaluation of various experimental machines of the

Ju 88-series in Dessau and Rechlin with particular regard to direct operational experience, proposed a type modification to the RLM in May 1941. The teams around Chief Designer Ernst Zindel and the project leaders Brunolf Baade, Bernhard Cruse and Karl-Ernst Schilling were forced to accept during the course of 1940/41 that on the one hand, the ongoing changes in terms of design and manufacturing techniques of the Ju 88-series were extremely time-consuming, whilst on the other, the project work on the Ju 90 long-range bomber and its follow-on models had to be instigated at short notice. As a result, enforced delays occurred in the development and testing of the Ju 288, which had to be agreed with the RLM.

In order to minimise this loss in time and to secure the required availability of new bombers based on the modification possibilities already submitted, Ernst Zindel proposed to State Secretary Generaloberst Erhard Milch the rapid development of an interim type based on the Ju 88 with its already improved combat qualities. The RLM, however, was not convinced of this proposal and expressed its doubts, considering that such a measure could eventually endanger the current assembly work on Ju 88 large-scale production that had just begun in Bernburg and could also conceivably tie up additional project capacity at Junkers. However, this did not turn out to be the case. The project leaders and their teams had so organised the necessary alterations that even significant design and technical innovations or improvements could be efficiently carried out without incurring any considerable losses in time.

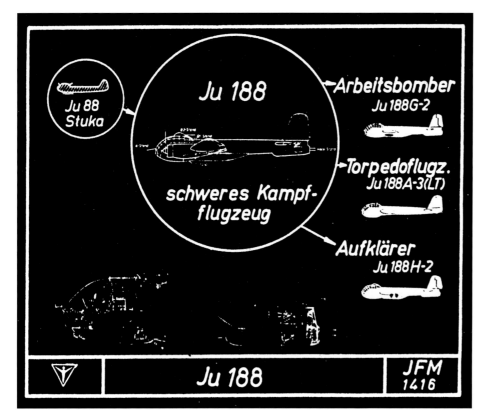

Ju 88 Stuka

Ju 188

schweres Kampf-flugzeug

Arbeitsbomber
Ju 188 G-2

Torpedoflugz.
Ju 188 A-3(LT)

Aufklärer
Ju 188 H-2

Ju 188

JFM
1416

Left: **The operational roles of the Ju 188. In smaller circle left: Ju 88 Stuka (dive-bomber); in circle at centre: Ju 188 heavy bomber; at upper right: Ju 188G-2 Arbeitsbomber (general-purpose bomber); at centre right: Ju 188A-3(LT) torpedo-carrier; at lower right: Ju 188H-2 Aufklärer (reconnaissance aircraft).**

Bottom: **The Junkers Ju 188E-0 (ST+GL) RLM communications and staff aircraft, 1943.**

In the meantime, the RLM had also recognised that the planned introduction date of the series-produced Ju 288 from August 1941 could no longer be met since the newly developed Jumo 213 engine had not yet reached series-production maturity. Pressured by Hermann Göring, Erhard Milch pressed the Junkers company leadership in Dessau for an immediate solution in the form of a proposed interim variant of the Ju 88 in place of the Ju 288

which was not yet ready for operational use. This, then, was the origin of the Ju 188 which, based on its new design and technical solutions and its resulting military-tactical configuration, would significantly improve on the previous medium bombers of the Luftwaffe in the future course of the war.

Erhard Milch took over the responsibilities of Generalluftzeugmeister following the enforced suicide on 17th November 1941 of GL-Chief

Ernst Udet who had been blamed by Hermann Göring for the Luftwaffe's planning failures. Milch soon became fully absorbed in his new post. From the JFM branch in Bernburg, which had just begun pre-series manufacture of the Ju 188E-0 at the beginning of 1943, he had Werknummer (airframe number) 10008 withdrawn at Dessau and converted with luxurious internal fittings as a communications and staff aircraft for the RLM. The aircraft's military callsign ST+GL signified STaff aircraft and General-Luftzeugmeister. Its maiden flight in the hands of Flugkapitän Hermann Steckhan took place between 1418 and 1442 hours on 27th February 1943.

This account has been necessary in order to describe the development of the economic and administrative aspects of the German aviation industry and in particular that of the Junkerswerke, based on available documents. At the same time it contradicts the widely published view held up to now, that the Ju 188 was a private development of the JFM in Dessau. On the contrary, it was precisely the abovementioned factors, some encouraging and some obstructive, that created the conditions that finally led to the development and production of the Ju 188.

Chapter Two

From Wind-tunnel to Conveyor-belt Manufacture

The Ju 188 Development Story

The first operational use of the Ju 88 occurred during the Western Campaign from May 1940, particularly in the air battles around Dunkirk and the attacks on British harbour installations. After the aircraft's range had been increased, its target sights were also aligned on ships in the English Channel, the North Sea and the Atlantic. Owing to its reliability and its tactical and technical parameters, as well as its many variants geared to the operational role, it had developed into the standard aircraft in the medium bomber class in a relatively short time.

In the summer of 1940, large-scale production of the Ju 88A-4 was under way in the newly erected assembly halls in the Junkers Bernburg plant that had been specially built for it. The plant, together with the nearby Junkers aero-engine facilities at Köthen and Magdeburg, was situated only 42km (26 miles) from the parent works in Dessau. Company-owned workshops and maintenance services at the most important forward airfields ensured a high state of operational readiness of the aircraft. Additionally, its solid construction and standardisation enabled a rapid exchange of manufacturing parts when necessary. The plant undertook all repair and servicing work on the aircraft, including the assessment of damage caused in battle or accidentally.

Not previously known in the history of the Ju 88 is that material testing of parts badly damaged in action was carried out in the JFM research laboratories in Dessau. This involved not only material samples received but also groups of parts and complete fuselage sections or engines. As a result of these strength tests, Junkers teams were able to make continual improvements to the Ju 88 on the design and material side. Patent rights protected a series of design modifications to the aircraft in the technological area of fittings as well as aerodynamic research. This was one of the most important and driving factors in the continual evolution of innovations, resulting in an improved aircraft that led to the Ju 188 and its successive models.

There was hardly an aircraft during World War Two that was so intensively and systematically wind-tunnel tested than the Ju 88 and its successors. There were also a surprisingly high number of experimental prototypes compared with similar aircraft developments, whether in the Third Reich or among the Allies.

With over 130 completed prototypes and test aircraft, not to mention mock-ups and special groups of airframe parts, the Ju 88 and its successor models were at the zenith of military aircraft research. What Dipl.-Ing. Philipp von Doepp and his team produced in the Junkers wind-tunnel in Dessau was not merely basic research but a continuous practical programme of research with the goal of constantly improving an aircraft as a weapons carrier in terms of both aerodynamics and performance.

If the development plan of the Ju 188 is considered from the aerodynamics aspect, two evolutionary processes become evident. One is the 1/25th-scale manufacture of models built of Caucasian walnut covered with innumerable down and wool tufts and tested in the wind-tunnel. The question as to which was the most effective aerodynamic form of the weapons stands was also thoroughly tested. The same held true for the aerodynamic shape of the entire engine cowling and nacelle for the BMW 801 and Jumo 213 powerplants. The entire 'Motorblock' of the Jumo 213 underwent aerodynamic investigation, and experiments were conducted with the BMW 801 cowling enclosure and the testing of external air induction ducts.

Another course was followed by a team centred around Dipl.-Ing. Manfred Strauss who, under the aegis of von Doepp, worked in the wind-tunnel until the occupation of the Junkerswerke by American forces on 21st April 1945. Although he was a 'Volljude' (100% Jew), he was able to escape the holocaust solely because of his high degree of specialist knowledge and ability, like other specialists of Jewish origin together with their families – about 50 individuals in all.

One of the principal tasks of the Strauss team was to investigate, by means of a series of aerodynamic tests, modifications to the wings and empennage surfaces in order to improve the combat capabilities of the aircraft, and in particular the Ju 188 and its successor models. Frau Dr. Eleonore Spieler-Witte was a member of the Strauss working staff between 1941 and 1945 and acted as test pilot 'Louis Witte' under Flugkapitän Friedrich Karl Maringer from 1942. She related to the author in August 1994: 'Onto a work table which consisted of a glass plate divided into several quadrants, numerous sheets of transparent

paper were stretched across for each test to be undertaken. The precise measurement readings were then entered onto them. This work table was located immediately beside the movable model in the wind-tunnel airstream so that the test could be observed continuously and in an emergency could be immediately stopped. To improve concentration on the model under investigation, it was partially illuminated by a cone of light. Thus, the behaviour of the wool tufts from eventual flow breakaway was more easily observed. The readings took the form of a series of dots whereby the curve joining them gave a picture of the airflow pattern. In this way, Philipp von Doepp and Manfred Strauss were able to evaluate the positive and negative forces acting on the model. Besides the normal aerodynamically favourable flight attitude, the extremely difficult phases encountered in air combat could be simulated which could present a deadly danger even to an experienced pilot. During works flight-testing and in the RLM E-Stellen (test centres), these wind-tunnel measurements were evaluated in practice. Even so, Philipp von Doepp time and again regretted the fact that some test pilots showed no interest in these valuable investigations.'

These tests also enabled the development groups of the design and materials research staff, taking into account the evaluation records of aircraft damaged at the Front, to improve structural safety and integrity and reduce weight. The co-operation between the individual working groups – wind-tunnel, materials evaluation, statics, design, experimental manufacture and flight testing – functioned like clockwork, so that only negligible delays were encountered.

The JFM in Dessau played a major role in the sphere of development of aero-engines and air-conditioned pressurised cabins for high altitudes. An important basis for this was the so-called 'stratospheric flights' that had been conducted mainly in the 1930s by Ju 49 and Ju 86P aircraft. The results of this research, begun under the direction of Hugo Junkers from 1929 onwards, were incorporated from 1940 by Dipl.-Ing. Justus Muttray in the design of the spherical and aerodynamically almost ideally shaped air-conditioned high-altitude cabin of the Ju 188. Together with a more powerful powerplant and a new type of turbosupercharger, it was temporarily possible to attain a

Above: **The Junkers Ju 88 V44 (NF+KQ) already displayed significant design features of the Ju 188.**

Photographs on the opposite page:

Top: **Rear fuselage mock-up from frames 23 to 33 for design and mechanical tests.**

Bottom: **The other side of the same wooden mock-up.**

ceiling of 12,000m (39,370ft). As a result, the Ju 188 and the later Ju 388 seemed predestined for use in the long-range reconnaissance role.

According to Junkers test pilot Rupprecht Wendel, who conducted flight trials on behalf of the RLM and especially with Ju 188 prototypes, the maiden flight of the Ju 188 V1, Werk-Nr. 10020, took place on 12th June 1943 at the parent works in Dessau. For this purpose, one aircraft was taken from the series-production line in Bernburg and modified in Dessau. In rare previously published literature concerning prototypes that could be ascribed to Ju 188 development, a number of seemingly contradictory flight dates have been given which, on closer examination, appear to have been based on the particular viewpoint of the author concerned. The much-modified Ju 88 V22 and V27

did not yet represent the Ju 188. They were, however, equipped with and tested component assemblies that were later used in the Ju 188. The basic structural features of the Ju 188 on the other hand are recognisable in the Ju 88 V43 and V44. The Ju 88 V61 to V63 also featured, to a greater or lesser degree, significantly complex design and configuration elements that are representative of the Ju 188. As an independent type, the Ju 188 used a number of prototypes in the Ju 88-series as a foundation for its development. Its ultimate configuration can be regarded as the result of a process of fluctuation between theoretical and practical knowledge assimilated between 1940 and 1942, as documented in the family tree of the Ju 188.

Besides wind-tunnel investigations and the 'flying test-beds' that led to practical tests with the prototypes, the JFM was also active in the field of materials research that was not simply confined to the laboratory. In the Sachsenbergwerft workshops in Dessau-Rosslau, on the bank of the River Elbe, there was a small department which despite its secluded location undertook important investigation work. Here, the works internal test series on technical design and airframe static load-testing, simulating an emergency let-down on water, were conducted. With the aid of various pieces of

apparatus, a whole series of conceivable loads were tested and evaluated on the airframe as well as on the wings and tail surfaces under extreme conditions of 'high seas damage'. A publication entitled *Junkers Erprobungsstelle in Trebbichau on the Elbe* which appeared in Stuttgart in 1973 probably refers to this department. The Trebbichau location near Köthen, however, does not lie on the Elbe and no traces of aviation history have been found there.

Under the designation Abteilung 700 (Department 700), a Junkers facility was built in the summer of 1943 on the military airfield at Brandis, northeast of Leipzig. Its task was to conduct clandestine flight trials with new prototypes, away from the ongoing mainstream war production. This company outstation was established out of the need to adequately protect intelligence of importance to the war effort during the course of increasing Allied air attacks from 1943 in the central areas of Germany. A standing contingent was established of some 70 individuals, increased in stages by skilled workers and specialists, which helped to lighten the workload of the company works testing group in Dessau. In this way, some Ju 188 prototypes underwent their flight trials in Brandis before being ferried to Rechlin to conduct further flight-testing – as related to the author by Junkers test pilot Rupprecht Wendel

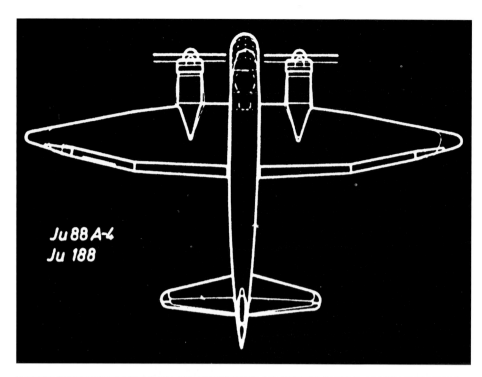

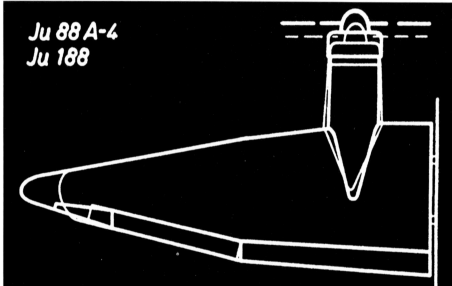

during a visit to the historic site in May 1995.

Understandably, flight testing resulted in damage being sustained as a result of malfunctions and during landings. These were unavoidable by the very nature of the activity, although every effort was made to minimise such incidents during later operational use. Even so, during a test flight on 17th September 1944 with Ju 188E-1, Werk-Nr. 260308 that had made its maiden flight on 27th October 1943, the aircraft crashed due to a maintenance error. The three airmen of the E-Stelle Rechlin's Technical Company, pilot Friedrich Diez, radio operator Richard Ecker and flight mechanic Kurt Günther, lost their lives.

Up until shortly before the entry of Soviet troops into Mecklenburg/Vorpommern in March and April 1945, pilots and technicians in various specialist fields worked on behalf of the RLM in Rechlin on experimental aircraft for the Luftwaffe. As late as March 1945, the 'flying test-beds' successfully carried out trials with the Jumo 213E (2,050hp/1,500kW) in a Ju 188, and the DB 603EB (2,550hp/1,655kW) in a Ju 88. By increasing the rpm and boost pressure to 2.0 atmospheres with the aid of a turbosupercharger and GM-1 (nitrous oxide) or methanol-water injection, the engine specialists were able to achieve significant improvements in performance. Surprising as it may seem, shortly before the end of the Third Reich, Germany had assumed an unchallenged lead over the Allies in the development of high-performance reciprocating engines. But this was not to have a lasting influence on the outcome of the war.

Comparative features of the Ju 88A-4 (thin outlines) and the Ju 188 (bold outlines).

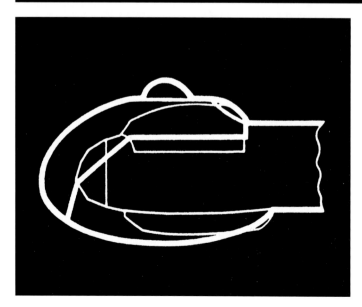

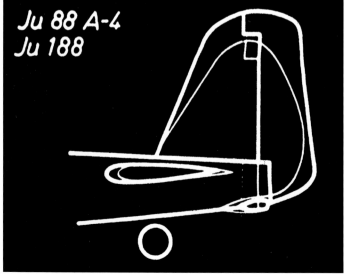

Chapter Three

Innovation Based on Experience and Knowledge

The Design of the Ju 188

The Ju 188 developed out of the Ju 88A-4 and the Ju 88B from 1941 as an optimum interim solution for the Ju 288 – a new development that was not yet ready for operational use. Retaining the basic design and main components, several working groups at the parent plant in Dessau logically developed and modified the aircraft type in such a way that its combat capabilities were significantly increased.

Military tactical experience and knowledge gained from direct frontline operations during the course of the war were used to create a combat aircraft that came to be used as a horizontal, glide and shallow dive-bomber. In modified form, the Ju 188 ultimately fulfilled the specialist roles of long-range reconnaissance and torpedo carrier.

The proven sheet-metal stressed-skin type of construction developed by the JFM in 1935/36 at Dessau was retained in the fuselage design of the Ju 188 – a further modification of the basic Ju 88 configuration. A detailed description of this type of construction has already been given by the author in an earlier book in this series devoted to the Ju 88, so only technical design details and basic alterations of interest to the modelmaker will be dealt with here.

The fuselage of the Ju 188 consists of a trapezoidal four-beam sheet-metal clad construction with frames and bulkheads arranged vertical to the longitudinal axis and subdivided into the fuselage forward, centre, and rear sections. All fuselage parts are made of duralumin alloy mainly fabricated as deep-drawn elements put together in successive stages, partly by using spot-welding of static non-load-carrying members mated together with rivets. Each fuselage component has its own static force circuit which, through the addition of construction elements in final assembly, forms a complete construction group for the aircraft.

The fuselage forward section with the cabin ventral flooring and removable cockpit canopy comprises the working area for the crew of four. Crew entry is via the hinged, lowered entry hatch in the cockpit floor known in the Ju 88 as the Bola [an abbreviation for Bodenlafette – a ventral gun-mount]. The rear portion of the cockpit roof is partially armour-plated, as is the hinged entry hatch. The cockpit can also be protected at the front and at the sides by armour plating. Compared to the Ju 88, the Ju 188 is better protected against enemy fire.

The fuselage centre section begins at transverse frame No 9 and ends at No 15. On grounds of statics, but also as a safety measure against enemy action or in an emergency situation, frame No. 12 divides the bomb-bay into forward and rear sections. Depending on the

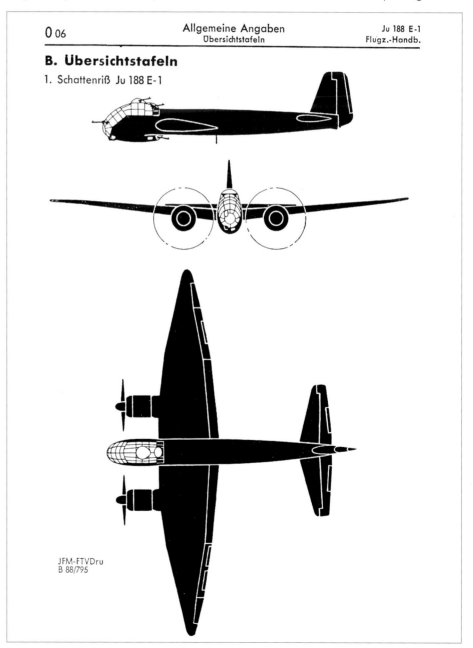

Right: **Ju 188E-1 three-view silhouette.**

2. Übersicht, Hauptmaße und Gewichte

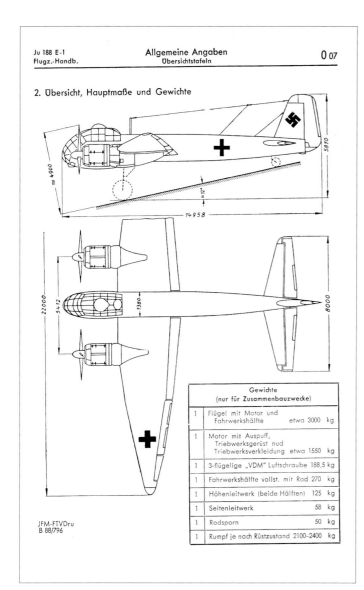

Gewichte (nur für Zusammenbauzwecke)		
1	Flügel mit Motor und Fahrwerkshälfte	etwa 3000 kg
1	Motor mit Auspuff, Triebwerksgerüst nud Triebwerksverkleidung	etwa 1550 kg
1	3-flügelige „VDM" Luftschraube	188,5 kg
1	Fahrwerkshälfte vollst. mit Rad	270 kg
1	Höhenleitwerk (beide Hälften)	125 kg
1	Seitenleitwerk	58 kg
1	Radsporn	50 kg
1	Rumpf je nach Rüstzustand	2100–2400 kg

JFM-FTVDru
B 88/796

3a. Bauteilebezeichnung und Zerlegbarkeit (Bild)

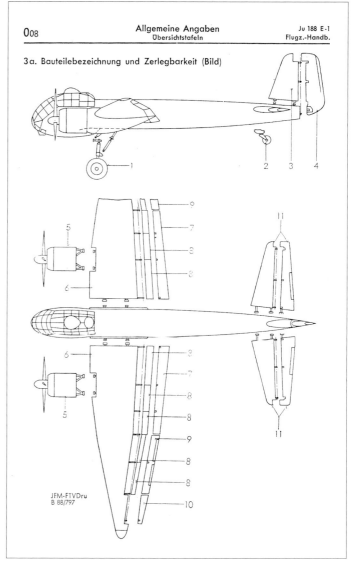

JFM-FTVDru
B 88/797

equipment carried, both halves of the bomb-bay can also be used for fuel storage. In keeping with their function, these spaces are accessible by means of doors on the underside.

The fuselage tail section, where the batteries, accumulators and the radio and safety equipment are installed, can be reached by means of a hatch in frame No 15 in the rear bomb compartment. The crew are able to access all fuselage segments over gangways.

The wings and tail surfaces with their respective control systems follow a similar pattern of construction to those of the Ju 88 but are of different surface areas and aerodynamic profiles.

Using examples from Junkers training department material, these differences are pictorially compared in order to illustrate their various configurations (see silhouettes on page 13). Ailerons and landing flaps employ the Junkers jet-slot principle.

The flying controls with longitudinal and lateral control surfaces are directed from a traversable control jamb housed in the centre fuselage with a movable arm for the control column. Rudder control is by means of a pair of movable foot pedals. Auxiliary control tabs assist the element

of control on all three axes. To reduce diving speed, dive-brakes which can be hydraulically extended and retracted are located on the wing underside. Pull-out from a dive is via an automatically operating trim correction mechanism. Dive-brake installation was later discarded.

The Patin PKS 11 course control is the early form of the present-day autopilot actuated by a servo-motor in the rudder controls. Even when one engine is inoperative, the aircraft is able to fly with this course control. With its complex network, the flight control system in connection with the powerplant represents an important step in the development of flight automation.

The 9-8801C-2 powerplant installation consists of two BMW 801G-2 air-cooled twin-row fuel-injection radials with two-stage superchargers, reduction gearing, rich-poor fuel-mixture switching, radiators for engine cooling having annular surfaces and the engine cowling. Each engine delivers 1,740hp on take-off at 2,700 maximum rpm. The three-bladed variable-pitch VDM dural propellers have a diameter of 3.7m (12ft 1⅝in) and a maximum blade width of 8%, the reduction gearing working in the ratio 13:24.

Above left: **Ju 188E-1 main dimensions and component weights.**

Above right: **Ju 188E-1 annotated major assemblies.**

Opposite page, clockwise from top left:

Ju 188E-1 description of the annotated parts.

Ju 188E-1 numbered access and maintenance hatches and ports.

The undercarriage mainwheels are housed directly behind the engines in the extended streamlined nacelles. Extension and retraction take place via a hydraulic pressurised oil system for the medium-pressure tyres. Each mainwheel can be individually braked. At the rear of the fuselage is a rotatable tailwheel.

The Baubeschreibung (Construction Description) of the Ju 188G-2 provides a graphic picture of a Ju 188 series-production model. It was only recently discovered through the estate of the late Flugkapitän Dipl.-Ing. Karl Werner Krüger. He had worked on it in December 1943 at the Junkers plant in Bernburg in his capacity as head of technical illustrations.

b. Bauteilebezeichnung und Zerlegbarkeit (Zusammenstellung)

Nr.	Benennung	Anschluß an	durch
1	Flugzeugbein mit Rahmen und Laufrad	Tragflügel	4 Zweikantbolzen
2	Spornrad mit Federbein-hebel und Radgabel	Rumpfende	3 Zweikantbolzen
3	Seitenflosse	Rumpfende	4 Kugelverschraubungen
		Seitenflosse und	2 Lagerbolzen mit Kronenmuttern an der Seitenflosse
4	Seitenruder	Rumpfende	1 Lagerbolzen mit Kronenmutter am Rumpfende
5	Triebwerksanlage	Tragflügel	4 Kugelverschraubungen
6	Tragflügel	Rumpfwerk	4 Kugelverschraubungen
7	Landeklappe	Tragflügel	3 Sechskantschrauben 1 Mutter M 8
0	Flügelendkasten	Tragflügel	(Nach Abbau der Landeklappen und Querruder) 5 Endkästen mit 1 x 10 u. 4 x 8 Sonderschrauben mit selbstsichernden Muttern
9	Querruder, innen	Tragflügel	1 Sechskantschraube 2 Muttern M 8
10	Querruder, außen	Tragflügel	1 Sechskantschraube 1 Mutter M 8
11	Höhenflosse mit Ruder	Rumpfende	4 Lagerbolzen (Wippe und Rumpfende) 8 Zweikantbolzen (Träger I und II) Leitung für Flossenenteisung, Trimmruderwellen 8 Sechskantschrauben (Ruder-Verbindungswelle) 4 Sechskantschrauben M 6 (Tr I und II)

Die Spaltverkleidungen um Rumpf/Tragflügel, Seitenflosse und Höhenflosse sind mit Flachrundschrauben, die Verkleidungsbleche von Tragflügel mit Senkschrauben befestigt. Stoßstangen, Seilzüge, elektrische und Drucköl-Leitungen sind vor dem Abbau an den vorgesehenen Stellen zu trennen.

---

b. Übersicht der Deckel und Klappen (Zusammenstellung)
(siehe auch Seite 013 und 014)

Nr.	Lage	Zweck	Befestigung
1	Rumpfseite rechts	Wartung der elektr. Kabel	Schnellverschluß
2	Rumpfseite rechts	Wartung der elektr. Kabel und Bediengestänge	Senkschrauben
3	Seitenflosse links	Wartung der Seitenflosse	Senkschrauben
4	Seitenflosse oben	Wartung der Antenne	Senkschrauben
5	Seitenruder rechts und links	Wartung des Trimmrudergestänges und der Federsteuerung	Schnellverschluß
6	Seitenruder unten	Wartung von Seitenruderantrieb	Senkschrauben
7	Rumpfende links und rechts	Wartung von Steuerseilen und Trimmruder-Getriebe	Schnellverschluß
8	Rumpfende links und rechts	Radspornbetätigung	Schnellverschluß
9	Rumpfende	Sammler-Einbau	Schnellverschluß
10	Rumpfseite links	Sanitätspack	Schnellverschluß
11	Rumpfseite rechts	Sauerstoff-Außenbordanschluß	Schnellverschluß
12	Rumpfseite rechts	Deckel für Seilrolle zum Heißen der Bomben	Schnellverschluß
13	Bodenwanne (C-Stand)	abwerfbarer Teil	Haltehaken
14	Einstiegklappe	abwerfbarer Teil	Rastbolzen und Gelenkbolzen
15	Rumpfseite links	Wartung der Bediengestänge, der Bedienseile und der Druckölleitungen	Senkschrauben
16	Rumpfseite links	Wartung des Bedientisches, vorn	Schnellverschluß
17	Rumpfseite links	Wartung der Seitenruderfußhebel (Abnehmen der Verkleidung)	Schnellverschluß
18	Führerraumdach vorn	Ausstiegklappe	Hebelverschluß
19	Rumpf-Unterschale	elektr. Außenbordanschluß	Gelenk
20	Rumpf-Oberschale	Deckel für Gurtkasten C-Stand	Schnellverschluß
21	Rumpf-Seitenwand links und rechts	Belüftungshutzen für vorderen Bombenraum	Gelenk
22	Rumpf-Oberschale	Aufhängung der Rumpfbehälter	Senkschrauben
23	Rumpf-Oberschale	Kraftstoff-Füllanschluß Rumpfbehälter (1. Behälterraum)	Senkschrauben
24	Rumpf-Oberschale	Wartung der elektr. Vorrats-messung (1. Behälterraum)	Senkschrauben
25	Rumpf-Oberschale	Wartung der elektr. Vorrats-messung (2. Behälterraum)	Senkschrauben
26	Rumpf-Oberschale	Wartung des Kraftstoff-Schnellablasses	Senkschrauben
27	Rumpf-Oberschale	Peilrahmenlagerung	Senkschrauben
28	Rumpf-Oberschale	Wartung des Seilzuges für Schlauchboot	Senkschrauben
29	Rumpf-Oberschale	Bootsklappe	Riegel-, Bolzen- und Hakenverschluß

---

noch b. Übersicht der Deckel und Klappen (Zusammenstellung)
(siehe auch Seite 012 und 014)

Nr.	Lage	Zweck	Befestigung
30	Rumpf-Oberschale	Wartung des Seilzuges für Schlauchboot	Senkschrauben
31	Rumpf-Unterschale	Wartung der Druckölleitungen am Spant 9	Senkschrauben
32	Rumpf-Unterschale	Drucköl-Füllanschluß	Schnellverschluß
33	Rumpf-Oberschale	Wartung des Kraftstoff-Schnellablasses	Senkschrauben
34	Rumpf-Oberschale	Kraftstoff-Füllanschluß für Rumpf-behälter (2. Behälterraum)	Senkschrauben
35	Rumpf-Unterschale	Bomben- oder Rumpfbehälter-klappen	Gelenk oder Senkschrauben
36	Rumpfende unten	Radspornklappen	Gelenk
37	Höhenflosse-Unterseite	Wartung d. Höhenrudergestänges	Senkschrauben
38	Höhenflosse-Unterseite	Wartung von Abfangvorrichtung und Höhenrudergestänge	Schnellverschluß
39	Höhenflosse-Unterseite	Wartung von Abfangvorrichtung und Höhenrudergestänge	Schnellverschluß
40	Höhenflosse-Unterseite	Wartung der Höhenflosse	Senkschrauben
41	Höhenflosse-Endkappe	Wartung der Höhenflosse	Senkschrauben
42	Höhenruder-Endkappe	Wartung des Höhenruders	Senkschrauben
43	Tragflügel-Oberseite	Wartung von Umfüllpumpe und Vorratsmessung	Senkschrauben
44	Tragflügel-Oberseite	Kraftstoff-Füllanschluß	Senkschrauben und Schnellverschluß
45	Abflußhaube oben	Schmierstoff-Auffüllung	Schnellverschluß
46	Tragflügel-Oberseite	Schmierstoff-Füllanschluß und Vorratsmessung	Senkschrauben
47	Tragflügel-Oberseite	Wartung von Umfüllpumpe und Vorratsmessung	Senkschrauben
48	Tragflügel-Oberseite	Wartung des Arbeitszylinders (Sturzflugbremse)	Senkschrauben
49	Tragflügel-Oberseite	Kraftstoff-Füllanschluß	Senkschrauben
50	Tragflügel-Oberseite	Tf. links Wartung des Schmierstoffvorratsmessers Tf. rechts Füllanschluß für Enteisungsbehälter	Schnellverschluß
51	Tragflügel-Oberseite nur im linken Tragflügel	Schmierstoff-Füllanschluß für Zusatzbehälter	Schnellverschluß
52	Tragflügel-Endkappe	Lösen der Endkappe	Senkschrauben
53	Flügelnase links (nur im linken Tragflügel)	Scheinwerferwartung	Gelenk und Senkschrauben
54	Abflußhaube oben	Steckerleitung für Fahrwerk-Endschalter	Schnellverschluß
55	Abflußhaube unten rechts	ermöglicht schnelles Lösen der Stoßstange	Schnellverschluß
56	Tragflügel-Unterseite	Wartung des Übersetzungsteiles	Senkschrauben und Schnellverschluß

---

noch b. Übersicht der Deckel und Klappen (Zusammenstellung)
(siehe auch Seite 012 und 013)

Nr.	Lage	Zweck	Befestigung
57	Tragflügel-Unterseite	Wartung des Steuerungsgestänges	Senkschrauben und Schnellverschluß
58	Tragflügel-Unterseite (nur rechter Tragflügel)	Wartung des Enteisungsbehälters	Schnellverschluß
59	Querruder links	Wartung des Trimmruder- und Federsteuerungsgestänges	Schnellverschluß
60	Tragflügel-Endkappe	Kabel-Kupplung	Schnellverschluß
61	Tragflügel-Verlängerung	Wartung der Steuerung und elektr. Leitung	Schnellverschluß
62	Tragflügel-Unterseite	Wartung des Tragflügels	Schnellverschluß
63	Tragflügel-Unterseite	Verschlußdeckel bei abgebautem Lastenträger	Schnellverschluß und Senkschrauben
64	Tragflügel-Unterseite	Wartung des Bombengestänges	Schnellverschluß
65	Tragflügel-Unterseite	Wartung des Schmierstoff-Zusatz-behälters u. Steuerungsgestänges	Schnellverschluß
66	Tragflügel-Unterseite	Wartung der Drucköl-Anlage für Sturzflugbremse und der Elt-Anlage	Senkschrauben und Schnellverschluß
67	Tragflügel-Unterseite	Wartung der Kraftstoffbehälter	Senkschrauben
68	Tragflügel-Unterseite	Schmierstoffablaß	Schnellverschluß
69	Tragflügel-Unterseite	Wartung des Schmierstoffbehälters	Senkschrauben
70	Tragflügel-Unterseite	Wartung des Kraftstoffbehälters	Senkschrauben und Schnellverschluß
71	Tragflügel-Unterseite	Wartung von Druckölleitungen, Triebwerksgestängen, elektr. Kabeln und Seilzügen für Heizung	Senkschrauben und Schnellverschluß
72	Tragflügel-Unterseite	Durchführung für Kraftstoff- und Druckluftleitung bei angebautem Lastenträger I bzw. Deckel mit Blindflansch bei abgebautem Lastenträger I	Senkschrauben
73	Abflußhaube unten	Fahrgestellverkleidung	Gelenk
74	Abflußhaube rechts	Wartung für Anlaß- und Zünd-anlage	Senkschrauben
75	Abflußhaube links	Kaltstartanlage, Zugang für Kugelverschraubung	Schnellablaß
76	Zwischenverkleidung	Wartung des Kaltstart-Absperr-hahnes	Schnellverschluß
77	Zwischenverkleidung	Wartung der Trennstellen am Triebwerk	Gelenk, Schnellverschluß
78	Triebwerksverkleidung	Verkleidungsklappen	Gelenk und Schnellverschluß
79	Triebwerksverkleidung	Kühlerhaube	Senkschrauben
80	Luftschraube	Luftschraubenhaube	Schnellverschluß

**JUNKERS FLUGZEUG-
UND MOTORENWERKE AG, Dessau**

Aircraft Manufacturing Plant, Bernburg Branch.
Short Construction Description No 141243.
Junkers Ju 188G-2 All-metal Land-based
Twin-engined Bomber.

Summary of Contents:

I. TECHNICAL OVERVIEW

1. Structure

In its overall structure the Ju 188G-2 conforms to Baubeschreibung (Construction Description) 100143 and the Ju 188A-2 supplement of July 1943. Principal differences are in the tail armament and bomb jettison equipment.

2. Usage

The Ju 188G-2 serves as a horizontal bomber or as a glide-bomber in a 30i angle of dive. The five crew members consist of four in the forward crew area and the tail gunner.

3. Equipment Condition

The term Rüstzustand (equipment condition) A, B, C or D can no longer be applied to this bomber because the Rüstsätze (field equipment sets) M1, M2, B1and B2 cannot be used. Whilst Rüstsatz M8 can be installed in the Ju 188, the M14 and M15 are not applicable. The following Rüstsätze can therefore be installed:

W1	=	A-Stand with MG 151
W2*	=	Coverings when the nose A-Stand is not installed
W5	=	B2-Stand with HD 151/2 [Heckdrehlafette = rearward-facing rotatable gun position]
W6*	=	Coverings when HD 151/2 is not installed
M8*	=	Bomb suspensions on port and starboard wings
B3	=	Lubricant auxiliary tank in port wing
Kuto*	=	Cable-cutting profiles as protection against balloon barrages

* These Rüstsätze are delivered only if specially ordered.

4. Delivery Items

These consist of the following Rüstsätze items installed:

W1	=	A-Stand with MG 151
W5	=	B2-Stand with HD 151/2
B3	=	Lubricating oil auxiliary tank in port wing

Delivery comprises the complete ready-to-fly airframe. Not included in the above and to be delivered by the customer are:

- the ready-for-use Jumo 213 powerplants
- the propellers
- the weapon equipment components
- the self-steering equipment
- the vibration-free compass equipment
- the aircraft wireless installations

Provision is made for the installation of these components and equipment in this delivery package. The items to be delivered by the customer are listed in a separate inventory.

II: FUSELAGE ASSEMBLY

1. Forward Fuselage

The fuselage forward section consists of the crew working area (cockpit) and extends from the fuselage nose up to fuselage transverse frame 8a. It accommodates the pilot, wireless operator, bomb-aimer and the C-Stand gunner (see upper silhouette on page 26). Emergency operation of the entry hatch as well as the shock absorbers is in a special ventral trough beneath the ventral gondola. The hand-lever for emergency operation is on frame 8. Visibility for the C-Stand gunner is improved by means of a port and starboard window in the ventral gondola behind frame 5. The storage battery location is between frames 4 and 4a beneath the platform. There are only two heated Nordland (Arctic terrain) windscreen panels in the cockpit, located in the upper portion of the canopy ahead of the pilot. The available heating panels on the windows between the pedals are not installed on the Ju 188A-2. The number of windowpanes between frames 1 and 2 is increased from one to three.

2. Centre Fuselage

The centre fuselage consists of Lastenräume (load-bearing compartments) I and II, extending from frames 9 to 12 and from 12 to 15. A fuel tank and weapons-release gear is installed in each compartment (see upper silhouette on page 26). The lower portions of frames 9, 12 and 15 are not installed. The only new addition is the right half of existing frame 15a. Beneath the load-carrying compartments are the bomb-bays extending from frames 8 to 20, together with the side panels and lower bomb doors. The forward side panels extend from frames 9 to 12 and the rear ones from frames 12 to 15a on both the left and right sides of the fuselage. On the guide beams for the bomb-bay doors the side panels are secured by quick-fasteners, so that mechanical operation of the side panels cannot occur. The bomb-bay panels, one each on the left and right side, extend from frames 9 to 15a, where each panel is supported and secured on three beams. The attachment points for these are on frames 9, 12 and 15a. Bomb door opening functions operate entirely electrically and hydraulically. The operating mechanism is attached to frame 15a and driven by an electromotor via drive shafts. The hydraulically operated activation cylinders are located on the right fuselage side wall between frames 10 and 11. By means of control rods, the movement of the drive gear is transmitted to the bomb-bay doors which form the entire covering of the fuselage skin. Suspension of the fuselage fuel tank, as on the Ju 188A-2, is on the supporting beams located on the top of the fuselage. Hydraulic operation of the landing flaps is set higher on frame 12 and protected by a safety grille.

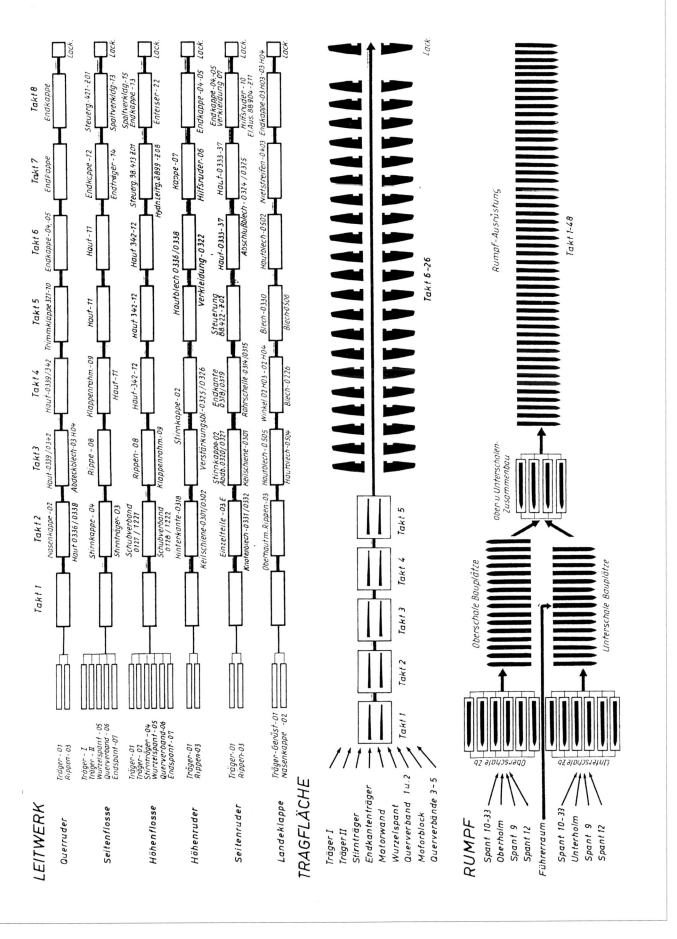

Sequential stages of the Ju 188 series-production cycle for the tail surfaces, wings, and fuselage respectively.

Endzusammenbau

Triebwerksrüste

1-2-3-4-5-6-7-8-9-10-11-12
1-2-3-4-5-6-7-8-9-10-11-12

Bereitstellung für den Endzusammenbau

Takt I
Rumpf auf Fahr-bühne, Seitenflos-se u. Seitenruder anbauen.

Takt II
Fläche lks u. rechts an Rumpf anschr. Höhenflosse anb. Rohrleitungen verbinden

Takt III
Landeklap.,Querrud. sowie Triebwerk an TF lks u.re anschr. Höhenruder an-bauen.

Takt IV
Spaltwerklg. für Höhenflosse u. Seitenfl.anbr. Be-dienanlage u.Querr-fen Hydr.Anl.pru-fen u.Verst-Luftschr aufziehen

Takt V
Steuerg.in Flächen versplinten Masch scharfgest Notflug f.Bomben u.Rauch betätig anschl. einst u.prüb.eren

Takt VI
Leitungen anschl Führerraum-Be-heizung,

Takt VII
Hilfsteistlstg.bei Endabnahme u zwar Prüfung der Elt.-Su-FT.v.An-Anlage

Takt VIII
Leitwerk u Spann-verklg anbr.Leitw-Eritesung anschr u.prüfen,Fertigungs-mangel beheb Maschine wiegen

J.185 86
5

18

3. Rear Fuselage

The rear fuselage extends from frame 15 to 32a. The tail armament position for the tail gunner extends from frame 30 to 32a where the traversable armament is attached (see the mock-up photograph on page 10). To accommodate the tail gunner's compartment, the fuselage depth from frame 25 has been increased. The transition to the trough type of enlargement takes the form of a covered hood. Entry to this position is through the door on the left-hand side and in an emergency it can be jettisoned in flight. To ease the tail gunner's exit after the door is jettisoned, a spoiler flap is opened into the airstream. An emergency tail-skid is situated between frames 32 and 32a, the fuel quick-release exit being located between frames 29 and 30.

4. Undercarriage

The main undercarriage and tailwheel have been strengthened. Mainwheel dimensions have been increased to 1220 x 445mm (48 x 17.5in) and the tailwheel to 630 x 220mm (24.8 x 8.7in) necessitating the installation of a new undercarriage cowling and modification to the extension housing. Tailwheel emergency operation can be effected from the tail gunner's position, consisting of a hand-pump located on the left side of frame 32, a hydraulic oil tank behind frame 30 and the corresponding conduits. The fuselage attachment point of the tail-wheel retraction strut has been relocated in front of frame 26 (see the mock-up photograph on page 10), new attachment points having been introduced for tailwheel covering-flap operation.

5. Empennage Surfaces

a) Elevators
With the lengthening of the fuselage, tailplane span has been correspondingly increased but its total surface area has remained unaltered. Owing to the presence of the rear crew entry door, the fuselage root portion of the elevator features a cut-out.

b) Vertical tail
The vertical fin up to the rudder position remains unaltered in comparison with the Ju 188A-2 but is reduced in height due to the increase in fuselage depth. The rudder also features a cut-out at the base to improve sighting for the rear gunner and is attached to the fin at three points.

c) Dive-brake lattices
The dive-brake lattices are not installed.

Illustration on the opposite page:
Final assembly sequences for the Ju 188.

6. Controls

As against the Ju 188A-2, installation of the tail gunner's position has necessitated an alteration to the control systems in the rear fuselage.

7. Wing

The wing is identical in plan form and construction to that of the Ju 188A-2. There are 20 spherical bottles for the oxygen system in the starboard wing. They are located between stringers I and II; 4 bottles are between ribs Vb and Vc and the remainder between Qv, V, and the end profile. For quick release of the fuel housed in the wing tanks, an exhaust outlet is located in the left and right wing halves.

III. POWERPLANT INSTALLATION

1. Powerplants

The entire installation is designated 8-1013B-2. The engine is the Jumo 213A-1, a twin-row inverted V 12-cylinder 4-stroke unit having fuel injection, water cooling, high-pressure blower, spiral throttle, automatic filling regulator, self-operating switch from the low- to high-altitude blower and vice versa, single-lever engine operating unit with stop position on the power lever (return from idling) and reduction gearing. The powerplants are delivered by the engine manufacturer ready for installation and operation.

2. Propellers

The propellers consist of fully automatic hydraulically operated three-bladed variable-pitch wooden Jumo VS 111 propellers of 3.7m (12ft 1⅝in) diameter and 9.5% maximum blade width.

3. Fuel System

For the fuel system, the following tanks are installed:
a) 2 inner wing tanks each of 415 litre capacity = 830 litres
b) 2 outer (auxiliary) wing tanks each of 425 litres capacity = 850 litres
c) 1 fuel tank in forward fuselage bay I of 725 litres capacity = 725 litres
d) 1 fuel tank in rear fuselage bay II of 700 litres capacity = 700 litres
Total fuel capacity = 3,105 litres

The fuel capacity can be increased by the carriage of two jettisonable tanks on the wing left and right suspension points I and II, each of 900 litres capacity, giving an additional 1,800 litres. Fuel tank pumps KBP 16L are situated at the filler heads of each tank. The quick-release conduit for the fuselage fuel tanks runs between the tailwheel and the tail armament position to the fuel exhaust port situated between frames 29 and 30. For the outer wing tanks, the exit for the quick-release fuel con-

duits lies between ribs Ivd and Qv IV beneath support II. Engine performance is monitored by means of an rpm indicator and fuel consumption indicator. The latter, operated electrically, is independent of the aircraft network and is therefore not subject to disturbances. It consists of:
e) an inductance indicator attached to the injection pump
f) an electrical current supplier driven by the engine equipped with crankshaft rpm
g) a fuel-consumption gauge in the cockpit which shows fuel consumption in litres/hour measured by the inductance indicator

4. Lubrication System

Owing to the fuel tanks installed in the fuselage load-carrying bays, an auxiliary lubricant tank is available as Rüstsatz B3, the system in the fuselage and wings being unaltered from that of the Ju 188A-2. Lubrication of the Jumo 213A-1 takes place through pressure-circulation via a main and auxiliary flow circulation system. The main flow lubrication system is understood to mean the main channels of the lubricating fluid within the engine, the auxiliary flow circulation having the task of replenishing the lubricant consumption and engine leaks. Lubricant fluid temperature is adjusted to that of the coolant. In the heat exchanger situated at the oil cooler location beneath the engine, the temperature of the oil flowing in the mainstream circulation is adjusted to that of the coolant. Lubricant pressure is regulated by a high-pressure relief valve.

5. Servicing System

The Jumo 213 power output, similar to that of the BMW 801, is governed by a power lever via a control device. A novelty is that with this power lever, a particular injection quantity can be selected and, by means of a corresponding regulator set to a particular air-fuel mixture ratio, can be automatically transmitted. The control unit regulates a) the rpm, b) the mixture, c) the ignition, d) the quick-stop mechanism, and e) the booster switch altitude. By activation of an engine magneto on the control unit via a key switch, it is possible to deliberately alter the switching altitude from high- to low-altitude (for economical cruising flight).

IV. EQUIPMENT

1. Electrical System

The two 6 DL6 electrical storage batteries are situated in the cockpit where the two heating panels are located. The drive motor for operating the bomb-bay doors is located at frame 17, the hydraulic struts being operated by a magneto valve. As this aircraft model does not have the Rüstsätze M1, M2, M14 and M15, the corresponding electrical support systems are accordingly deleted.

2. Wireless Installation

The aircraft wireless installation system consists of the following:

a) FuG 10P with transmitter and receiver equipment for the long- and short-wave range
b) BZ 6 with target direction-finding receiver
c) TZG 10 auxiliary telephone apparatus in the short-wave range
d) FuG 16 aircraft-to-aircraft system in the short- and long-wave range
e) FuG 25a IFF
f) FuG 101 landing altimeter
g) Fu Bl 2F blind-landing system

The antenna winch and the antenna shaft with a jack attachment and the Asch 10 setting indicator are not installed. The tail armament position and crew intercom is connected by means of the ADB 12 connecting box. Like the other series-production models, the Ju 188G-2 also has the S-compass installation. The master compass is relocated in the rear fuselage between frames 24 and 25.

V. SAFETY INSTALLATIONS

1. High-altitude Oxygen System

The 20 spherical oxygen bottles are located in the right wing, with four bottles available for each crew member. With the exception of the additional supply for the tail gunner, the distribution arrangement of the breathing equipment is identical to that in the Ju 188A-2.

2. Safety and Rescue Installations

For the pilot, radio operator and tail gunner there are seat-cushion parachutes, and for the bomb-aimer and C-Stand gunner, back-strap parachutes. All crew members have a parachute waistbelt harness, the pilot and rear gunner having an additional shoulder harness.

Depending on its mission, the aircraft can be equipped with a dinghy or desert emergency equipment or a winter emergency equipment set. These items, however, do not form part of the standard aircraft equipment delivery package.

3. Heating and De-icing Systems

The engine exhaust gases are used for cockpit heating and wing and tail surface de-icing. As opposed to the Ju 188A-2, the heating system is expanded to include the tail gunner's position, the latter connected by a tube to the warm-air circuit for tailplane de-icing. De-icing of the wing and tailplane leading edges is by means of warm-air heating. Propeller de-icing utilises de-icing fluid which is directed sideways to the variable-pitch arms of the propeller hub.

Photograph on the opposite page:
Two-layer assembly platform for the Ju 188 rudders in the ATG Leipzig license plant.

4. Hydraulic System

This serves to operate the following items:
a) the undercarriage mainwheels and tailwheel
b) the landing flaps
c) the altimeter
d) the bomb doors

Instead of the electrically operated Klauber and Simon valves, magnetic valves are installed.

VI. WEAPONS STATIONS

The bomber has five weapon Stände (positions):

1. A-Stand

On the right-hand side of the cockpit canopy roof is a semi-fixed forward-firing MG 151/20 in the L 151/3 turret. The weapon has a left-oriented ammunition feed, electrical loading and mechanical priming. The full-belt container located in frame 2 houses 200 rounds. The dive-sight serves as the target-aiming device when the weapon has been centred and trained onto a target.

2. B1-Stand

In the jettisonable part of the cockpit roof is a large lens-shaped LLG 131 gun-mount and an upward-firing traversable MG 131A-2 machine-gun. The MG 131 has a right-hand-oriented ammunition feed, hand trigger and electrical priming. Two full-belt containers each with 500 rounds are available for this weapon. One ammunition container is located on the left and the other on the right fuselage wall between frames 6 and 8a.

3. B2-Stand

The B2-Stand is installed as Rüstsatz W5 and consists of the hydraulically operated rotatable HD 151 turret equipped with the MG 151/20 which has a right-hand ammunition feed, electrical triggering and electrical priming.

4. C-Stand

In the C-Stand (ventral gunner's position) is an MG 131B-2 with right-hand ammunition feed, a hand trigger for hand loading and electrical priming. A WL 131 AR roller gun-mount serves for positioning. The ammunition container is attached above the MG on to frame 8 and holds 500 rounds.

5. H-Stand

Two MG 131s with a magnetic trigger and a hand loader are installed in the tail-gun position, the ammunition being primed electrically. The weapons are superimposed in the HL 131Z twin-turret and operated by the tail gunner. Target alignment is by means of a Revi (Reflexvisier = reflector gunsight). Each MG 131 is provided with 600 rounds housed in a full-belt ammunition container behind frame 15

and led by feedbelts to the weapons (see upper illustration on page 32). The long feed-path necessitates a belt-feed drive motor located between frames 28 and 29. By loss of the feed drive motor, the belt-feed system can be hand operated.

VII. WEAPONS

1. Jettisonable Weapons

These consist of:
a) the weapon supports in the forward loading bay, and
b) the suspension rails in the rear loading bay

In addition, the wings have the attachment points for the M8 load supports to the left and right. The 'Blindscharfgestänge' is not installed.

In the forward loading bay there are three side by side suspension beams between frames 9 and 12. The central supporting beam is for a single 500/1000 bomb mount; the two outer ones are intended for a double 500/1000 mount. In the rear bay is a grid for the attachment of two 500/1000 bomb mountings.

When handed over, the aircraft contains:
c) in the left and right supports of the forward loading bay a Schloss 500/XII bomb mounting
d) on the central support in the forward loading bay a Schloss 2000/XII bomb mounting, and
e) on the grid in the rear loading bay, two Schloss 500/XII bomb mounting clasps.

2. Targeting Equipment

The targeting apparatus installed for bomb release is the BZA-1, and attachments are also available for the installation of a Lotfe 7C or Lotfe 7D telescopic bombsight and a Navi 3 in the aircraft. These items can be installed as needed by the agency owning the aircraft.

VIII: EXTERNAL SURFACE PROTECTION

Until the issue of new documentation, the exterior surface protection is applied as with all production variants of the Ju 88 and Ju 188 according to the Ju N 52004.0-04 list. The same applies to the Ju 188G-2 in the normal two-tone black-green (70)/dark green (71) on the upper surfaces and night camouflage on the fuselage underside.

For night camouflage, the following colours are used:
a) intermediate varnish 7123.99
b) black colour 7124.22, and
c) thinner 7205.00

Instead of the previously used external Flieglack (dope) 7122, Flieglack 7150 is applied. For internal coating, Flieglack 7121 is used.

IX. MAINTENANCE AIDS

The Betriebs-Hilfsgeräte (working aids or tools) are subdivided into:
1. Implements and special tools – primary
2. Implements and special tools – secondary
3. Auxiliary implements

Items under 2. and 3. do not form part of the standard aircraft delivery set and are supplied separately by the RLM. Those items delivered with the complete aircraft are as follows:

1. Primary implements/contents

a) In the Bordsack (aircraft toolkit) are the following protective coverings:
- one for the pilot's cockpit and crew canopy
- two for the engines
- one for the pitot tube
- one each for the mainwheels
- one for the tail gunner's position

In addition there are:
- 2 anchoring lines 20mm in diameter and 2.5m in length
- 2 fixing brackets for the ailerons
- 3 fixing brackets for the empennage controls
- 1 movement excess-pressure press
- 2 steel-wire tubes for the oil pressure press
- 1 oil-tight bag for the grease press and steel-wire tubing

Also contained in the Bordsack are a set of engine tools delivered by the engine manufacturer, consisting of:
- 1 tyre-pressure gauge with tubing for pressures from 1 to 5.5 atmospheres
- 1 combination pliers c.160mm in length
- 1 screwdriver of c.4mm cutting width and c.180mm in length
- 1 screwdriver of c.8mm cutting width and c.360mm in length
- 1 mechanic's hammer of 250 to 300g weight
- 1 monkey-wrench adjustable for widths from 0 to 15mm
- 1 monkey-wrench adjustable for widths from 0 to 30mm
- 1 tube wrench (Becro-Polygrip) of c.250mm length
- 1 'Edu-Drill' screwdriver with recoil spring in handle, 50cm long
- 1 Junkers toolset for milled slits in countersunk screws for drill screwdriver
- 1 sheet-metal box for housing small items
- 1 small roll insulation tape of 10m length in sheet-metal case
- 1 small roll of galvanized safety wire of 10m length and 1mm diameter, and
- 1 cowling key for the VS 11 airscrew spinner.

Above: **View of the cockpit and canopy with its metal bracing frames.**

Opposite page: **Junkers Jumo 213 Engine Summary Portfolio of December 1944, with photograph of the Jumo 213A-1.**

Key to summary columns:

Triebwerks-Gerät-Nr.	*Powerplant equipment number*
Motor Gerät-Nr. *RLM*	*engine designation*
Zelle	*Installed in airframe*
Luftschraube	*Airscrew designation*
spät(er)	*later*
Bemerkung	*Remarks*
Bombertriebwerk	*Bomber engine*
Jägertriebwerk	*Fighter engine*
Axialkühler	*Axial radiator*
Einheitskühlerkopf	*Centralised radiator head*
Schmierstoffvorrat	*Lubricant content*
1100, 1150, etc	*diameter in mm*

Stand Dezember 1944

Übersicht der Serientriebwerke mit JUMO 213

Triebwerks-Gerät-Nr.	Motor Gerät-Nr.	Zelle	Luftschraube	Bemerkung
9-8013 B2	9-213 A 1	Ju 88/188	VS 111	Bombertriebwerk Axialkühler 1300 ⌀
9-8213 E1	9-213 AG1	FW 190 D9	VS 111	Jägertriebwerk Axialkühler 1100 ⌀ Schmierstoffvorrat im Triebwerk
9-8213 D1	9-213 E 1	Ju 88/388	VS 9 spät. VS 19	Bombertriebwerk Einheitskühlerkopf 1150 ⌀
9-8213 FE1	9-213 E 1	Ta 152 E	VS 9 spät. VS 19	Jägertriebwerk Einheitskühlerkopf 1150 ⌀
9-8213 FH1	9-213 E 1	Ta 152 H	VS 9 spät. VS 19	Jägertriebwerk Einheitskühlerkopf 1150 ⌀
9-8213 H1	9-213 F 1	FW 190 D11 und D12	VS 9	Jägertriebwerk Axialkühler 1100 ⌀; Schmierstoffvorrat im Triebwerk

Jumo 2636

23

DEUTSCHES REICH

AUSGEGEBEN AM
14. SEPTEMBER 1942

REICHSPATENTAMT

PATENTSCHRIFT

№ 725 100

KLASSE **62** c GRUPPE 5 01

J 58408 XI/62 c

❊   **Dr.-Ing. Otto Mader in Dessau-Ziebigk**   ❊

ist als Erfinder genannt worden.

Junkers Flugzeug- und -Motorenwerke AG. in Dessau

Einrichtung zur selbsttätigen Veränderung der Flügelblattsteigung mehrerer nicht gleichachsig
angeordneter Verstellluftschrauben

———

Patentiert im Deutschen Reich vom 24. Juni 1937 an

Patenterteilung bekanntgemacht am 30. Juli 1942

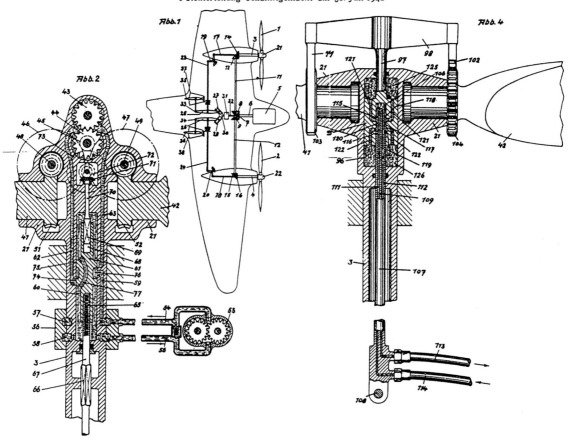

**Junkers Patent No 725100 for a self-operating airscrew pitch-change installation on twin-engined
aircraft, applied for on 24th June 1937 and publicised on 30th July 1942.**

DEUTSCHES REICH

AUSGEGEBEN AM
24. SEPTEMBER 1942

REICHSPATENTAMT

PATENTSCHRIFT

№ 725524

KLASSE **62**b GRUPPE 5 06

J 62756 XI/62b

❋ **Max Lange in Dessau-Roßlau** ❋

ist als Erfinder genannt worden.

Junkers Flugzeug- und -Motorenwerke AG. in Dessau

Einrichtung an Fließfertigungsstrecken für den Flugzeugbau

Patentiert im Deutschen Reich vom 30. Oktober 1938 an

Patenterteilung bekanntgemacht am 6. August 1942

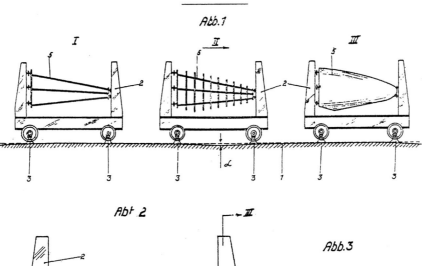

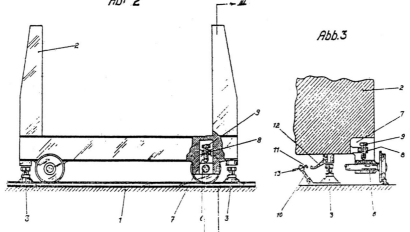

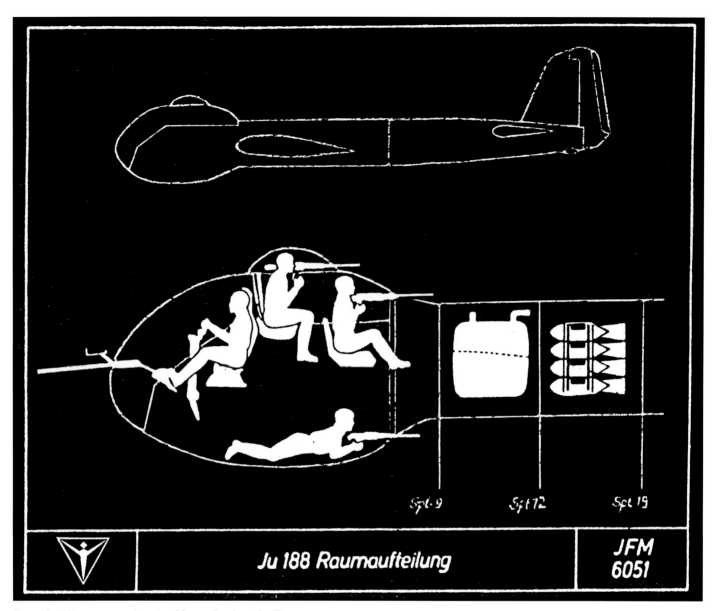

Ju 188 Raumaufteilung

JFM 6051

Above: **Ju 188 crew compartment and forward and rear loading bays – side view.**

Below: **Ju 188 crew compartment – top view**

Below: **Ju 188 Rüstsätze (standard equipment sets) for: Betriebsstoff = fuel and lubricants; Munition = ammunition; Waffen = weapons.**

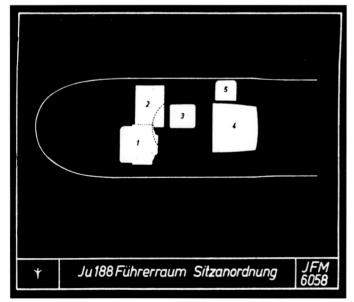

Ju 188 Führerraum Sitzanordnung

JFM 6058

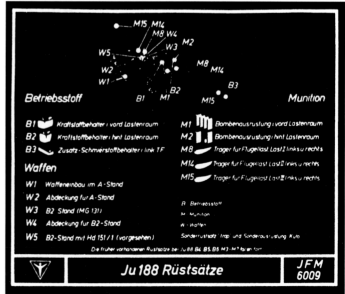

Ju 188 Rüstsätze

JFM 6009

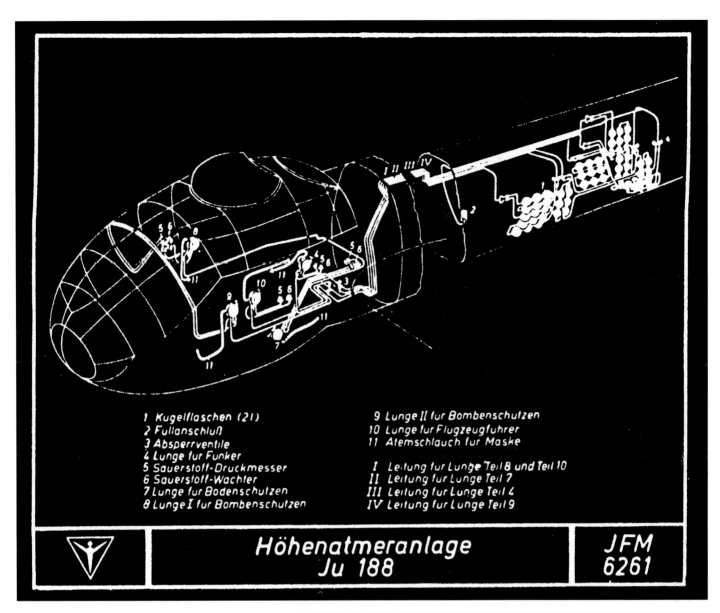

1 Kugelflaschen (21)
2 Fullanschluß
3 Absperrventile
4 Lunge fur Funker
5 Sauerstoff-Druckmesser
6 Sauerstoff-Wachter
7 Lunge fur Bodenschutzen
8 Lunge I fur Bombenschutzen

9 Lunge II fur Bombenschutzen
10 Lunge fur Flugzeugfuhrer
11 Atemschlauch fur Maske

I Leitung fur Lunge Teil 8 und Teil 10
II Leitung fur Lunge Teil 7
III Leitung fur Lunge Teil 4
IV Leitung fur Lunge Teil 9

**Höhenatmeranlage
Ju 188**

**JFM
6261**

Above: **Ju 188 high-altitude oxygen system components.**

	Rüstzustand A		Rüstzustand B		Rüstzustand C	
Flugstrecke km	1300	2900	2400	3450	3300	3800
Kraftstoff ltr.	1680	3480	2900	4700	3580	4480
Bomben kg	3000	1400	2500	1000	2000	1000
Abfluggew. kg	14570	14475	14985	15070	15085	14895

Die Flugstrecken sind errechnet für eine Reisegeschwindigkeit von 400 km/h in H=6 km

**Ju 188 Errechnete Flugstrecken
bei verschiedenen Rüstzuständen**

**JFM
6010**

Right: **Ju 188 Rüstzustand (equipment composition)
A, B, C, with corresponding:**

**Flugstrecke = range in km;
Kraftstoff = fuel in litres;
Bomben = bombload in kg;
Abfluggewicht = take-off weight in kg.**

**Range in each case is for a cruising
speed of 400km/h at 6,000m (248mph at 19,685 ft).**

RLM/GL/C-E 2/II	JFM-FTM	Kobü-Ltg.K-Techn.Ltg. BAL	Febü	BAL	Werwe
RLM/GL/C-B 2/II	JFM-FTV-Au	Kobü-Rh K-Kaufm.Ltg./TWL	Feprü 2x	TWL	Rela
E'St.Rechlin	JFM-FVZ	Kobü-Elt Buchhaltung KWL/	Werwe 2x	KWL	Rewe
E'St.Tarnewitz	JFM-Zentral-	Kobü-Wa Av	Rewe	Rela	Av 2x
	einkauf	Kobü-Tw	Belei I		Feprü
	JFM-FTV-Dru		Belei II		

Junkers Flugzeug- und Motorenwerke A.G.   Bernburg, den 17.Dezember 1943
    Flugzeugbau Zweigwerk Bernburg   Kr/Ha.
        FG-K, TB/IV

FG.
Bauanweisung
Ju 188 G-2

ab Werk-Nr. 210061

KA.-Nr.:   71 88 10 10 / 014
Termin: lt. FG-AV-Plan

Bauausführung:

Der Bauausführung liegt die Baubeschreibung Ju 188 E-1 u. F-1 Nr. 100143
mit Nachtrag I und Anhang für Ju 188 A-2 u. D-2 Flugzeuge sowie die an-
liegende Kurz-Baubeschreibung für Ju 188 G-2 Bomber vom 14.12.43 zu
Grunde.

Bordfunkanlage:

Der Gerätesatz der Blindlandeanlage Fu Bl 2 F ist nicht einzubauen.

                                        FG-Block K, TB
                                     Technischer Vertrieb

                                        [signature]

Anlage:
1 Kurz-Baubeschreibung

Right: **Ju 188 electrical installations in the rear fuselage.**

Illustration on the opposite page:

Cover page of the Ju 188G-2 manufacturing instructions issued by the JFM AG, Bernburg, dated 17th December 1943 and applicable from Werk-Nr. 210061 onwards.

Number Key to the Ju 188G-2 Kurz-Baubeschreibung
(Short Construction Description) on pages 30 to 32

Page 30, for Ju 188G-2

1. A-Stand with MG 151
2. B1-Stand with MG 131
3. B2-Stand with MG 151
4. C-Stand with MG 131
5. Two storage batteries
6. Fixed antenna mast
7. 725 litre fuel tank in forward fuselage bay
8. 700 litre fuel tank in rear fuselage bay
9. Direction-finding (D/F) installation
10. Ammunition belt containers for tail gun
11. Drive for control surfaces
12. AAG 2 antenna tuning equipment
13. W/T rack
14. W/T rack
15. Master compass
16. Transformer station
17. Drive for elevator trim
18. Correction calculator
19. Airspeed signal indicator
20. BK-drive
21. Relay containers
22. AAG 25a antenna adjustment equipment
23. Fuel collector tank of 415 litres capacity
24. Lubricant tank
25. 425 litre fuel tank
26. Fuel quick-release orifice
27. Auxiliary lubricant (Rüstsatz B3)
28. FuG 101 receiver
29. FuG 101 transmitter
30. Transformer
31. Oxygen system spherical bottles
32. Wing de-icing
33. Elevator de-icing

Page 31, for Ju 188G-2 and H-2:

1. Tail gunner's seat, adjustable for cruise, combat and emergency exit positions
2. Activation lever for seat adjustment
3. Back and head cushioning
4. Shoulder harness
5. Waist harness
6. Cabin roof padding between frames 30 and 32
7. Cabin roof padding between frames 32 and 32a
8. Padding on frame 32
9. Knee padding, adjustable
10. Shoulder padding, adjustable
11. Head padding
12. Chest support harness
13. Dorsal armour plating
14. Lateral fixed armour plating
15. Side adjustable armour plating
16. Forward armour plating
17. Ventral armour plating
18. Oxygen controller
19. Oxygen pressure gauge
20. Breathing apparatus
21. Switch panel
22. Intercom connection box
23. Ignition transformer
24. Interference eliminator
25. Ammunition-round counter
26. Entry door, jettisonable
27. Airflow deflection flap
28. Door jettison lever and flap release
29. Tank for hydraulic oil and tailwheel emergency activation
30. Hand-pump for tailwheel activation

Page 32, for Ju 188G-2 and H-2

I. Armament (upper drawing)
1. Ammunition container for lower tail gun
2. Ammunition container for upper tail gun
3. Ammunition feed channels
4. Feed drive with motor and hand operation
5. Connection for hand operation
6. Rockers
7. Contacts for belt-feed motors
8. Ikaria turret
9. Guide rollers
10. MG 131s
11. Weapon steering
12. Revi gunsight
13. Revi steering mechanism
14. Armoured-glass panel

II. Control Mechanisms (lower drawing)
15. Rudder motivation mechanism of course control
16. Rudder control push-rods
17. Double-lever shaft
18. Control lever axle
19. Lever axle for elevators with raised rudder shaft
20. Rudder cable pulley on fuselage
21. Cables leading to rudder
22. Cables for elevator activation
23. Elevator control balance
24. Elevator push-rod
25. Elevator crankshaft
26. Elevator hydraulic strut
27. Connecting arms

III. Tailwheel Mechanisms
28. Tailwheel
29. Sprung strut
30. Load bearing arm
31. Hydraulic strut
32. Tailwheel door operating rod
33. Left door flap

IV. Fuel System
34. Quick-release conduit
35. Fuel outlet

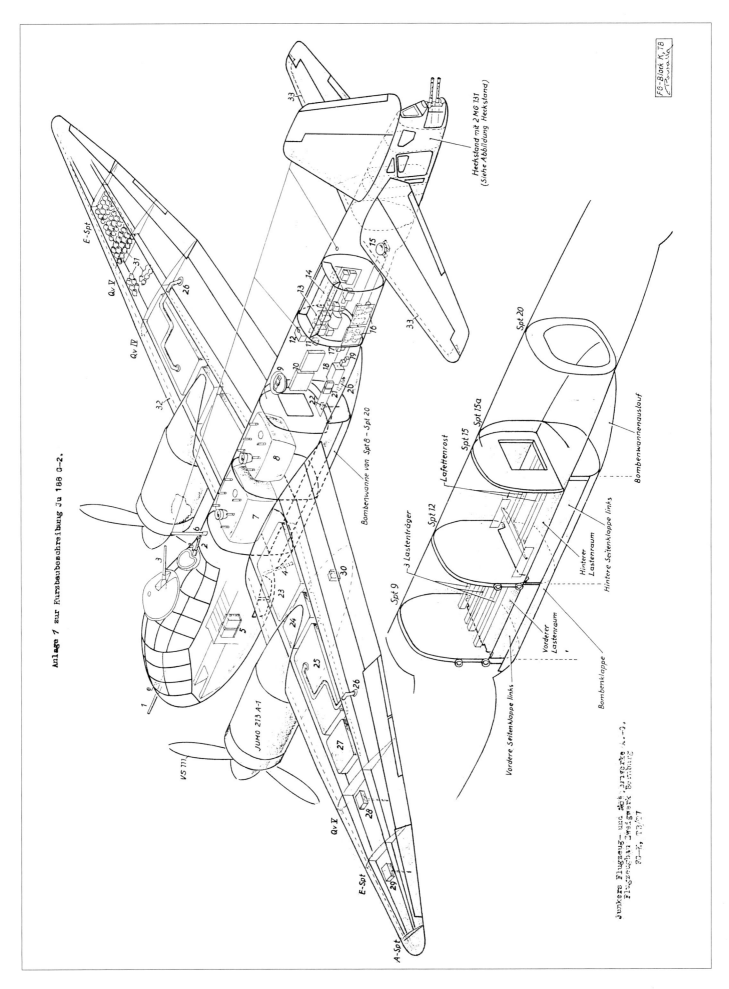

Anlage 7 zur Kurzbaubeschreibung Ju 188 G-2.

Heckstand mit 2 MG 131
(Siehe Abbildung Heckstand)

Bombenwanne von Spt 8 - Spt 20

Spt 20

Spt 15 15a

Spt 15

Lafettenrost

Spt 12

3 Lastenträger

Spt 9

Hintere Lastenraum

Vorderer Lastenraum

Bombenwannenauslauf

Hintere Seitenklappe links

Vordere Seitenklappe links

Bombenklappe

JUMO 213 A-1

VS 111

Junkers Flugzeug- und Mot.,Werte A-2,
Flugzeugbau Zweigwerk Bernburg
FG-2, T3/57

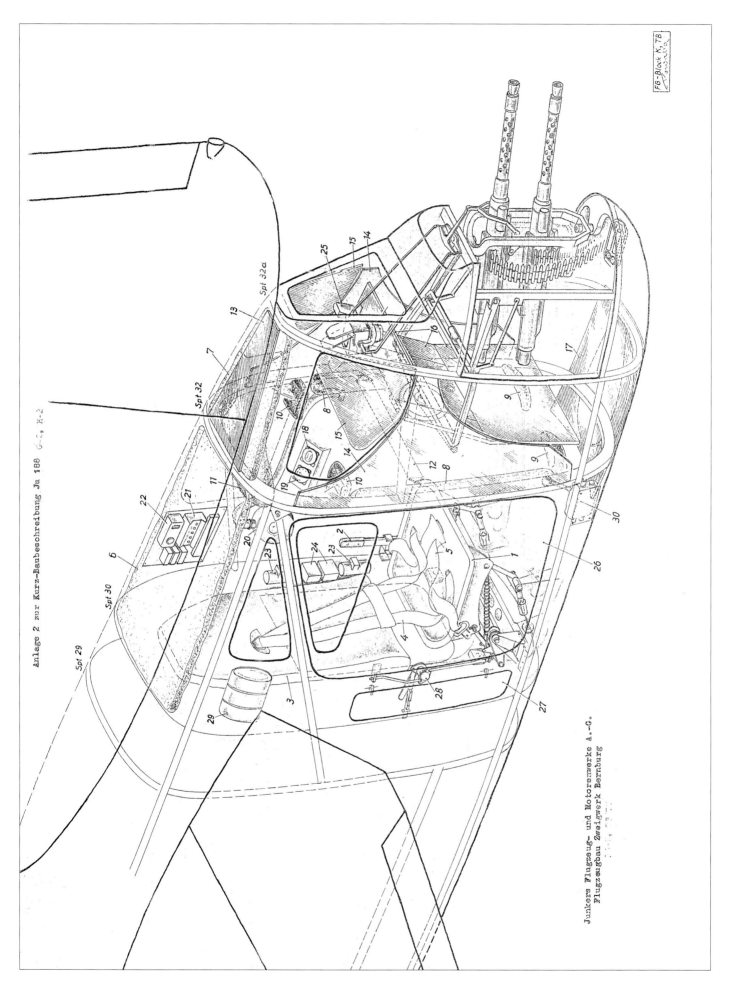

Anlage 2 zur Kurz-Baubeschreibung Ju 188 G-2, H-2

Junkers Flugzeug- und Motorenwerke A.-G.
Flugzeugbau Zweigwerk Bernburg

F6-Block K, TB

31

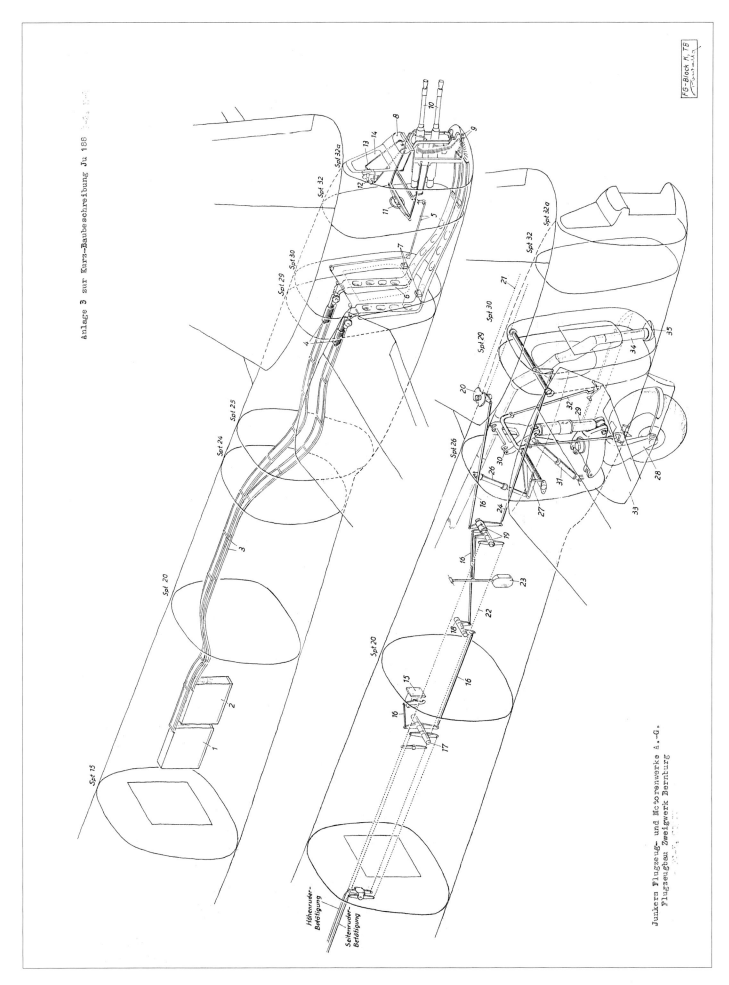

Anlage 3 zur Kurz-Baubeschreibung Ju 188

Spt 15

Spt 20

Spt 24

Spt 25

Spt 29

Spt 30

Spt 32

Spt 32a

Spt 26

Spt 29

Spt 30

Spt 32

Spt 32a

Spt 20

Höhenruder-
Betätigung

Seitenruder-
Betätigung

FG-Block K, TB

Junkers Flugzeug- und Motorenwerke A.-G.
Flugzeugbau Zweigwerk Bernburg

Chapter Four

Operational Theatre

The Many Variants of the Ju 188

Following the defeat of the British Expeditionary Force near Dunkirk on 4th June 1940, the Battle of Britain was expected to provide a yardstick against which to measure the Luftwaffe's weapon technology in its flying formations. Priority was given not only to the pilots' flying skills but also to the quantitative and qualitative aspects of the aircraft.

Only a few weeks later, on 16th July 1940, Adolf Hitler signed the order authorising Operation *Sea-Lion* which signalled the beginning of preparations for the offensive against the British Isles. For this, the Luftwaffe had been assigned a special role. The combat formations were not only to interrupt the supply connections to the sea but were also to destroy the centres of arms production, military bases, dockyard installations and the radar early-warning system – the so-called Chain Home stations.

After Hitler's 'Peace Note' of 19th July 1940 to England had remained unanswered by Winston Churchill, an air battle began which was pursued by both sides right from the start with an indescribable determination and stamina. At the beginning of the air battles there were 1,400 aircraft on the German side, notably the Dornier Do 17Z, Heinkel He 111H and He 111P as well as the Junkers Ju 87 and Ju 88; on the British side there were some 800 aircraft consisting mainly of Spitfires and Hurricane fighters. This situation altered in the course of time. Whereas at first the British fighter squadrons flew to meet the Luftwaffe over the English Channel or over the North Sea, the RAF air defences later allowed their opponents to penetrate deep into the homeland. Only then did the defences open up, forcing the German pilots to disengage due to lack of fuel in order to be able to return to their bases. Tactically, the bomber echelons could now fly successful combat missions only during surprise twilight or night sorties. From the summer of 1941, most Luftwaffe formations were assigned to operate on the Eastern Front against the Soviet Union and in the Mediterranean against the British combat formations. Those remaining in the West continued their air attacks on dockyards along the British coast and up as far as Scotland. However, the principal targets still within range of German aircraft engaged in attack or mine-laying operations were ships in the Atlantic, the Channel and the North Sea.

The theatre of war was now expanding relentlessly in both Europe and Africa. On 1st September 1942 the OKW-Report (OKW = Oberkommando der Wehrmacht [Supreme Command of the Armed Forces]) appended remarks on the following geographical locations: 'South of the lower Kuban – south of Stalingrad – south-west of Kaluga – south of the Ladoga Sea – in the high north of Norway – south of Alexandria and to the northwest of Cairo...'! The political and operational misjudgements of the OKW clearly came to the fore, but it was also evident that air warfare had its technical and logistical limits. The tactical depths of penetration of the aircraft were limited and their capacities were already exhausted in the field of air transport, particularly at the 'Flying Front'. New paths had to be followed.

A Ju 188 F-2 ready for take-off.

Reichsmarschall Hermann Göring therefore pressed the aircraft industry in ever-stronger terms to meet these demands through new developments and type modifications as well as by increasing production quantities. Added to that was the need to categorise aircraft in accordance with their intended mission. It is truly astonishing to consider the scale of the development of the Ju 88 programme and that of its successors in the JFM in Dessau, with its extensive range of individual large-scale manufacturing series comprising more than 60 variants. Even when a few variants were completed only as prototypes, considerable time and effort were spent on them. The question thus inevitably arises: How was all this feasible?

A central control developed in the JFM at Dessau co-ordinated the entire airframe and engine programme. Included in it were not only its own aircraft and engine plants but also the licencees with their plants, the repair facilities and the subcontractors. The Dessau parent plant with its development and experimental manufacture served as a model enterprise. With this degree of control, logistically planned down

Opposite page: **A Ju 188A-2 being prepared for a sortie. Mounting the bombload served as motivation training for the operations crew.**

Below: **Ju 188 G-0 experimental variant with manned tail turret.**

to the smallest detail in which all possible obstacles had been taken into account and therefore almost eliminated, it was successful in achieving the greatest German aircraft construction programme with almost military precision.

In the 1930s the American ocean-flyer Charles Lindbergh had visited Germany several times. He was naturally interested mainly in German aviation industrial centres and spent some time in Dessau. In his memoirs he repeatedly praised the scientific and technical know-how of the Junkerswerke, which he described as the best of its kind. This was of importance, because after the entry of American troops into central Germany in the spring of 1945, he pointedly visited the Junkers parent plant at Dessau and robbed it of its famous scientific library and patent collection.

In response to a directive by Erhard Milch, a study undertaken by the RLM into how the Luftwaffe could improve its tonnage figures of shipping sunk was confirmed in June 1942 by the implementation of improved flying techniques. As a consequence, the GL-Conference of 29th July 1942 favourably considered use of the Ju 188. It was faster, more manoeuvrable and had a greater operating radius with regard to depth of penetration than the Ju 88-series and the Do 217. For combating sea targets in the North Sea, it was expected that at least one Ju 188 Gruppe could be operated from March 1943. This planned action, however, was

delayed since the Jumo 213 engine was not yet ready for operational use. Besides the increased motivation of the pilots, their performance capabilities also improved with the implementation of new weapons technology. Hence the order to 'target the east coast in an orderly manner as the east coast is the most fruitful area for operations, presupposing that the fighters can be warded off' was consistently followed by those pilots tasked with attacking shipping targets.

With the commissioning of the Ju 188A, the flying units had hoped for a considerable improvement in the deteriorating air situation apparent since 1941. But the more powerful Jumo 213 already mentioned was still not sufficiently advanced for operational use. Recourse had therefore to be made to the BMW 801G-2 (the 9-8801C-2 with VDM airscrews) which thus placed the Ju 188E-series ahead of it. The Ju 188F long-range reconnaissance aircraft also entered series production in parallel. It was only after this that the Ju 188A-series equipped with the Jumo 213 followed.

In February 1943, the first Ju 188E pre-production aircraft left the Bernburg assembly lines equipped with the BMW 801G. Although less powerful than the later Jumo 213 engine, it was considered satisfactory by the RLM and sent for service trials from May onwards. In October 1943, the Ju 188E-1 took part in its first large combat operation on the Western Front

Right: Data sheet for the Ju 188E-1 bomber, reconnaissance and torpedo carrier.

Hand-written data are as follows:

Engines:	**2 x BMW 80IG-2**
Take-off power:	**2 x 1,740hp = 3,480hp**
Wingspan:	**22.00m (72ft 2⅛in)**
Length:	**14.96m (49ft 1in)**
Height:	**4.90m (16ft 1in)**
Loaded weight:	**14,000kg (30,864 lb)**
Take-off speed:	**175km/h (109mph)**
Cruising speed:	**385km/h at 300m**
	(239mph at 984ft)
Range:	**1,100 to 2,400km**
	(683 to 1,491 miles)
Take-off length:	**650m (71yds)**
to 20m (66ft)	**1,100m (3,609ft)**
Fuel consumption at economical power:	
at 500m (1,640ft)	**260 litres/hr per engine**
at 4,000m (13,120ft)	**270 litres/hr per engine**
Oil consumption:	**6 litres/hr per engine**

with I/KG 6 in combination with Ju 88s. Its employment on special tasks as a fast long-range reconnaissance aircraft able to operate at high altitudes and on shipping attack missions as a tactical torpedo carrier allowed the Ju 188 to undertake missions over the Atlantic and the North Sea.

Development of the Jumo 213, one of the best high-performance aero-engines ever built, was the responsibility of Dipl.-Ing. August Lichte. He had designed especially for this engine a new fuel feed regulator operated by a single lever that proved to be outstanding. Although over 9,000 of these engines had come off the production lines between 1943 and 1945, losses repeatedly occurred due to the war situation. As a result of an RLM directive, the engine suspension points on the Ju 188 were so configured that either BMW or Jumo powerplants could be attached. The dive-bombing requirement was later removed from all series-produced aircraft in favour of an increase in speed, albeit marginal. The period of dive-bombing had long passed and the Luftwaffe adapted itself to the altered air combat situation.

The Ju 188 was used in operations between the Mediterranean and the deep fjords of the high northern Scandinavian area. The tropical equipment, the sea distress equipment and the winter equipment therefore formed part of its standard conversion kits. Besides the already

mentioned air-conditioned pressure-tight spherical crew compartment, to cater for the operational theatre the cabin hood was fitted with sun protection blinds or else heatable panels when used in the high northern territories. A further safety measure was the provision of a separate oxygen system for each crew member. An important element was the aircraft instrumentation, which included the bomb-aiming and weapon installations, the radar and auxiliary equipment for night flying, and the radio and crew intercom including the radio homing systems which in air combat provided an additional safeguard for the crew. With the aircraft's good handling qualities, and even under extreme weather conditions, the pilots were able to exploit the Ju 188's favourable combat characteristics combined with their piloting skills and daring in some sectors of the front which had yet to be secured.

Despite its military successes in operations against enemy sea targets and in support of ground troops, the Ju 188 was only a medium-class bomber with which there were often parallel developments in the aviation industry. For example, the Heinkel He 219 appeared as a competitor in the night-fighter role. A turning point in the air war from 1942 at the latest could have been achieved only with strategic long-range four-engined bombers, but these were not yet operational. From the time when the Ju 188 was accepted by the Luftwaffe and put into service, the responsible generals in the RLM had underestimated the logistical requirements that would be placed on the ground organisation and in particular upon the support services. Compared to the Ju 88, the space requirement for maintenance technology at service airfields rose by 100%. This applied equally to the newer developments by other manufacturers. Structural measures were also

called for such as additional depots and storerooms, as well as considerable runway extensions that were necessary especially for the He 177 and the later Messerschmitt Me 163 and Me 262.

An attack planned for the beginning of 1945 as part of Operation *Drachenhöhle* (Dragon's Den) by II./KG 200 on Scapa Flow with 15 'Mistel' (Mistletoe) composites and several bomber squadrons, among them the Ju 188, had fallen victim to the weather. A weather front approaching from the Atlantic caused the attack date to be repeatedly put off. Under these circumstances, the RAF exploited the favourable wind direction for the British bombers and the thick, low cloud cover. In low-level attacks they destroyed the 'Mistel' composites, which were difficult to hide because of their size, as well as a number of bombers that were still in place at their operating base.

At the end of February 1945, Junkers technicians at the combat airfield near Ballerstedt in the Harz region were able to realise a plan on which they had set all their hopes, but which would not in fact have an effect on the outcome of the war. In addition to the ongoing 'Mistel' production at Junkers, concentrated mainly in the northeastern part of the Harz mountains between Nordhausen/Kohnstein and Halberstadt/Aschersleben, still further variants were to have been built. There thus appeared the so-called 'Mistel 4' combination, consisting of a Ju 188 explosives-filled lower component and an Me 262 piloted upper component as the guidance aircraft. These did not, however, reach the flight test stage as the required Jumo 004 turbojets were not available on time. Immediately before the arrival of American troops, the 'Mistel' composites were blown up by the aircraft technicians, in compliance with orders, in the presence of two Wehrmacht officers.

Photographs on the opposite page:

Top: **Ju 188 F-1 reconnaissance version.**

Centre: **Head-on view of the Ju 188 F-1.**

Bottom: **A Line-up of Ju 188s on a combat airfield in Norway, summer 1944.**

Junkers Ju 188 E-1

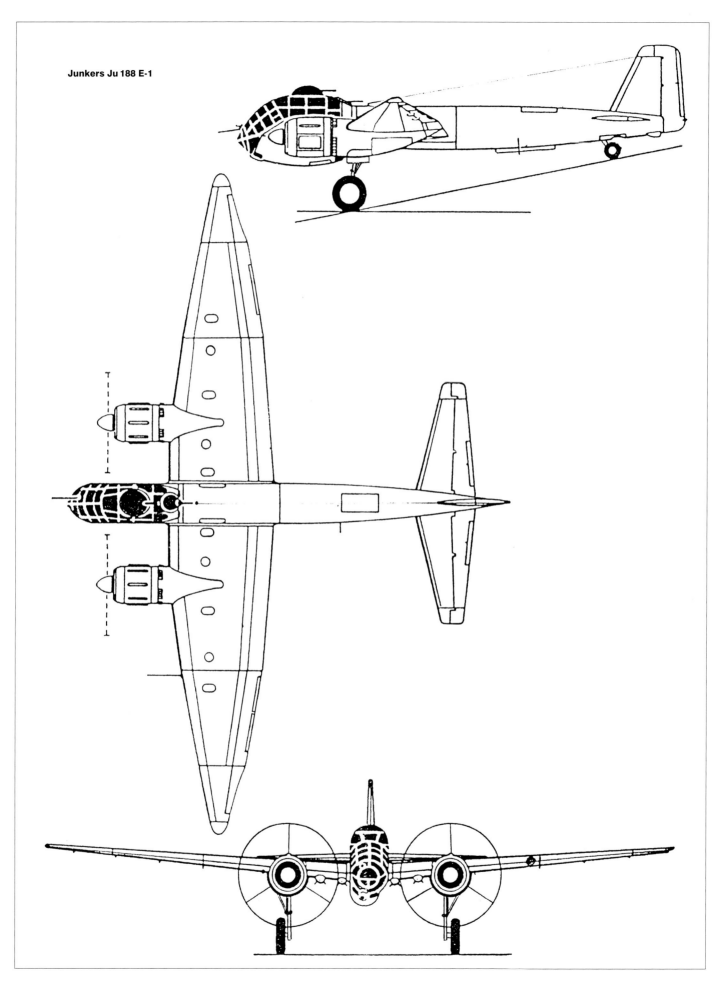

Junkers Ju 188 D-2

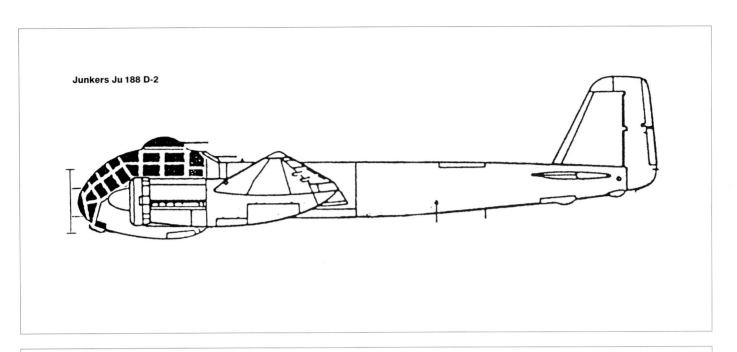

Junkers Ju 188 F-1

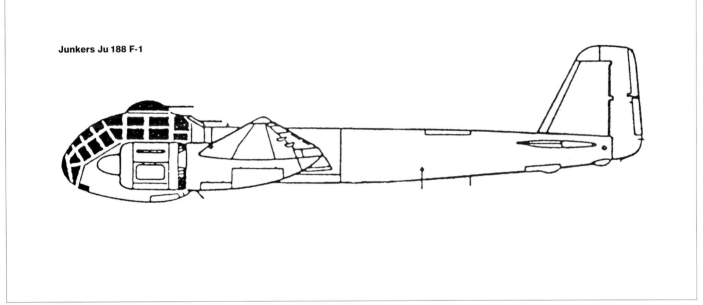

Junkers Ju 188 G-0

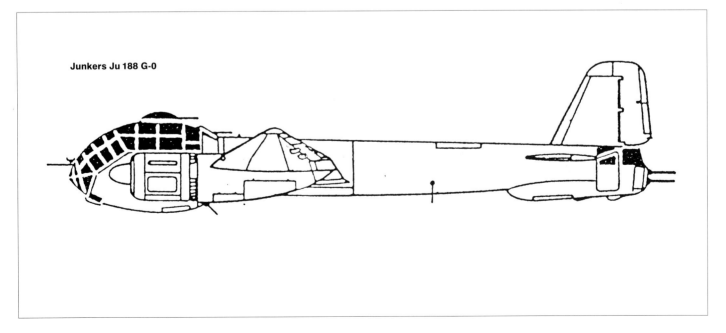

Chapter Five

The Genealogy of the Ju 188

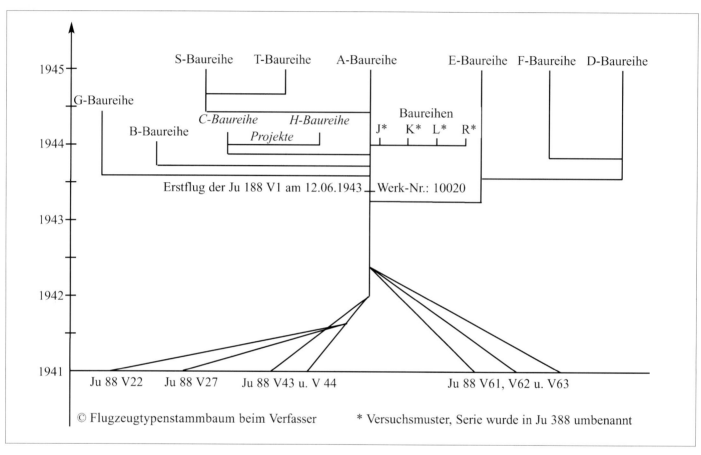

The first flight of the Ju 188 V1 (Werk.-Nr.10020) was on 20th June 1941. On the lowest line are the various related Ju 88 prototypes which preceded it. * The J, K, L and R-series were redesignated as the Ju 388.

The Ju 188 Series Data

Version	Role	Powerplants	Remarks
SERIES A			
Ju 188A-0	Level bomber	2 x Jumo 213A-1 2 x 1,776hp at t.o. and 2 x 1,600hp at 5km (16,400ft)	Pre-production variant. The A-series entered production after the E-series. Bombload was 16 x 65kg bombs in fuselage 2 x 1000kg or 4 x 500kg bombs on ETC underwing suspensions
Ju 188A-1	Level bomber	2 x Jumo 213A-1	As A-0 but with built-in dive-brakes. Did not enter series production.
Ju 188A-2	Level and dive-bomber	2 x Jumo 213A-1	Conformed to the A-0 series but with improved engine performance, ie auxiliary fuel injection system and VS 111 variable-pitch propellers.
Ju 188A-3	Level bomber	2 x Jumo 213A-1	As A-0 but laid out as torpedo carrier with 2 x LT 1B each of 800kg or 2 x LT 5Fb each of 765kg weight.

Version	Role	Powerplants	Remarks
		SERIES B	
Ju 188B-2	Level and dive-bomber	2 x Jumo 211J 2 x 1,420hp	As A-2 but with lower-powered engine and correspondingly reduced bombload. Fall-back series if Jumo 213 was not available.
		SERIES C	
Ju 188C-0	Level bomber	2 x Jumo 213A-1	Mock-up corresponding to A-2 but with enlarged rear fuselage in this area as it served as model for a remote-controlled H-Stand with 2 x MG 131s. Did not enter series production.
		SERIES D	
Ju 188D-0	Long-range reconnaissance	2 x Jumo 213A-1	Pre-series model without A-Stand armament. Had two auxiliary 300 litre drop-tanks and crew of three.
Ju 188D-1	Long-range reconnaissance	2 x Jumo 213A-1	As D-0, laid out for maximum range 3,400km (2,113 miles) and maximum speeds of 480-540 km/h at 6,000m (298-356mph at 19,685ft).
Ju 188D-2	Long-range reconnaissance	2 x Jumo 213A-1	Corresponded to D-0 but intended for sea reconnaissance role and equipped with FuG 200 'Hohentwiel' radar installation.
		SERIES E	
Ju 188E-0	Level and dive-bomber	2 x BMW 801ML 2 x 1,600hp	Pre-series model, equipped same as Ju 88A-4 but with the a new-vision cockpit, increased wingspan and crew of four.
Ju 188E-1	Level and dive-bomber	2 x BMW 80IG-2 (9-8801G-2 with VDM airscrews) Armament was: A-Stand: B1-Stand: B2-Stand: C-Stand: For both B-Stands an additional belt-feed with 500 rounds could be used. Bomb supports were:	Balloon cable-cutters on fuselage nose and on wing leading edges. 1 x MG 151 with 2mm barrel for fixed and movable firing in a gimballed suspension; 250 rounds. 1 x MG 151 in lens-shaped turret; ammunition 500 rounds. 1 x MG 131 in a rotatable turret; ammunition 500 rounds. 1 x MG 81Z in a rotatable turret; with 1000 rounds per gun. M1 (forward loading bay) M2 (rear loading bay) M8 (left and right) with Schloss 500 or 1000 to 2000 respectively. M14 with ETC 500.
Ju 188E-2	Level and dive-bomber	2 x BMW 801G-2 2 x 2,365hp	As E-1 but cockpit enlarged and raised on pilot's side; frame 8n moved to the rear, altered control attachment on frame 9, and altered B-2 and C weapon Stands. Armament as in A-3. Strengthened undercarriage.
		SERIES F	
Ju 188F-0	Long-range reconnaissance	2 x BMW 801G-2	As D-0, except for cameras as in Ju 88D-1 but with improved optics.
Ju 188F-1	Long-range reconnaissance	2 x BMW 801G-2	As D-0; armament as E-1. Engine unit 9-8801C-2 with VDM airscrews.
Ju 188F-2	Long-range reconnaissance	2 x BMW 801G-2	As F-1 but with modifications as under E-2 and FuG 200 'Hohentwiel' radar.

Version	Role	Powerplants	Remarks
SERIES G			
Ju 188G-0	Level bomber	2 x Jumo 213A-1	Experimental, conforming to A-2 but with modified and strengthened rear fuselage for manned tail gun position. No series production.
Ju 188G-1	Level bomber	2 x Jumo 213A-1	As G-0 but without manned tail gun position, replaced with 2 x FA 15 tail turret.
Ju 188G-2	Level bomber	2 x Jumo 213A-1	Prototype, as G-0 but with ergonomic H-Stand and new bomb jettison equipment.
Ju 188G-3	Level bomber	2 x Jumo 213A-1	As G-1 but intended as torpedo carrier. Armament as A-0.
SERIES H			
Ju 188H	Long-range reconnaissance	2 x Jumo 213A-1	Conformed to C-version but as improved project with increased range.
SERIES J			
Ju 188J	Zerstörer and night-fighter	2 x Jumo 213A-1 or 2 x BMW 801J-0	Project in weight-reduced form was built as Ju 388J.
SERIES K			
Ju 188K	Level bomber	2 x Jumo 213A-1 or 2 x BMW 801J-0	Project for a fast level bomber, later built as the Ju 388K.
SERIES L			
Ju 188L	High-altitude reconnaissance	2 x Jumo 213E 2 x 1,750hp	Project for a high-altitude and reconnaissance aircraft for day and night operations, built later as the Ju 388L.
SERIES R			
Ju 188R	Night-fighter	2 x Jumo213E-1 or 2 x BMW 801J-0	Project specially conceived for night operation with additional 'Schräge Musik' (Jazz Music) oblique upward-firing weapons. Was to enter series production as the Ju 388R.
SERIES S			
Ju 188S	Fast bomber	2 x Jumo 213C-1 or 2 x Jumo 213E-1	In configuration as A-2 but with redesigned full-view canopy as with later Ju 388K and increased engine performance.
		Bomb supports:	M1 (forward loading bay) M2 (rear loading bay)
		Armament:	1 x BK 5 in ventral trough as fixed forward-weapon. Special anti-tank project.
SERIES T			
Ju 188T	High-altitude reconnaissance	2 x Jumo 213C-1 or 2 x Jumo 213E-1	Project for an improved high-altitude and long-range recce aircraft. No series production.

Chapter Six

An Exemplar of Technocracy

The Ju 188's Armament

At a large propaganda meeting at the Berlin Sportpalast on 5th June 1943, Albert Speer in his role as Reichsminister for Armaments and War Production announced: 'We shall make available to the frontline a number of new weapons, new tanks, aircraft and submarines that will enable our fighting men to possess an unsurpassable superiority over our enemies to endure the battles ahead and will bring about ultimate victory.'

Important parts of this speech were repeated over the Junkers works intercom, both in the parent plant and in the branches. Extracts were also published in the Junkers magazine *The Propeller*. Many employees were able to recall this event even 50 years later and recounted how, in their daily work schedules which sometimes involved a 12-hour stint, they were able to

meet additional workload targets despite the continual Allied bombing raids. It was a difficult period, and each worker was acutely aware that the fate of Germany depended on achieving these goals set by Albert Speer.

These employees in the armaments industry fully understood the importance of their 'position on the home front' and exerted all efforts not only to meet but often to exceed the ever-higher demands they were set. Much had yet to be accomplished, especially in the field of flight techniques and armament, as it was imperative to regain air superiority at the frontline. Although in some sectors of the front the Luftwaffe was still partly in control, seen as a whole, however, it was already a lost cause. Air superiority was to be the crucial factor in determining the future outcome of the war.

It is therefore understandable that during the GL-Conference on 19th July 1943, at which fast-bomber planning up until 1949 was discussed, the General Staff Chief of the Development Office responsible for aircraft, Oberst Georg Pasewaldt, in the presence of Erhard Milch and other high-ranking experts, remarked that '...in the years 1945 and 1946 we will be reliant upon the Ju 188 in this class of equipment. We shall not obtain any relief either from larger aircraft, as these are too few; or from the faster aircraft that are necessary, as their range and bombload capacities are reduced. I place navigational and similar considerations in abeyance, although difficulties still exist in this sphere. I am also of the opinion that we need the medium bomber in its most refined form especially in the next three years.'

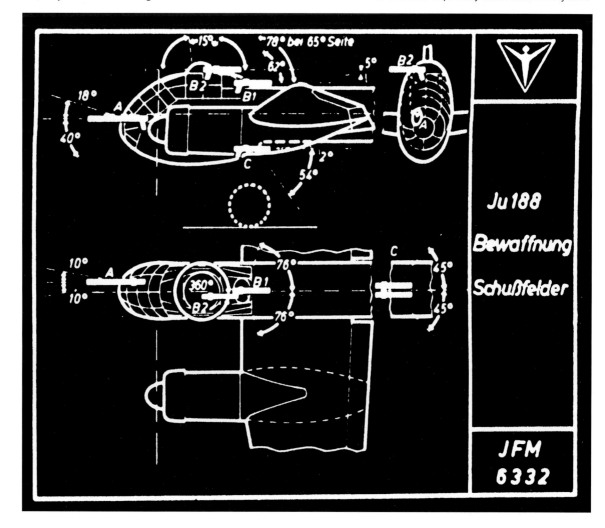

Ju 188 armament positions and fields of fire.

These remarks again highlight the miscalculations that had been made concerning the tactics employed by the Luftwaffe. The hesitant attitude of the RLM and the General Staff, and in particular the obstinacy of Adolf Hitler and Hermann Göring, would inevitably lead to insurmountable problems. The German offensive posture adopted from the beginning of the war changed from 1942/43 to a defensive one, which led to a review of strategic policy in an attempt to reverse the high losses being suffered at the Front. For this reason, the further development of the Ju 88 into the Ju 188 from 1941 onwards took on an urgent importance.

Alongside continual improvements to the powerplants, armament became the highest priority. Advances made in the mechanisation or automation of the technology, the calibre, and the rate of fire become apparent when comparing the Ju 88 weapon carriers from 1940 to 1944 and the Ju 188 in 1942/43. The original rate of fire was an average of 750 rounds per minute, but this was eventually raised to over 1,400 rounds per minute. Added to that were the improvements to the weaponry in terms of the effectiveness of its penetration and fragmentation effect. From 1944 there were even proposals for the design and testing of rocket-propelled weapons containers to be installed in the forward fuselage of the Ju 188 and Ju 288.

Dipl.-Ing. Gustav Steuerlein was responsible for this work on perfecting airborne weapons technology in the Design Department at the Junkers parent works in Dessau. This also involved measures for crew protection against enemy action. The installation of armour-plated sliding panels in the internal areas of the cockpit protected the crew against shrapnel from enemy bullets. However, these protective measures naturally resulted in a loss in aircraft speed and payload, and were therefore only partially introduced depending on the tactical use of the aircraft. In addition, aerodynamic investigations were conducted in the wind-tunnel in order to minimise turbulence which unavoidably led to a reduction in speed and affected the aircraft's flying behaviour in certain circumstances.

One of the main objectives in this review of the weapons arrangements was to achieve deflection-free projectile release. Tests had shown that when firing at right angles to the line of flight, above a particular airspeed, trajectory deflections occurred that could not always be compensated by a sighting adjustment. Assistance was provided by a small metal surface in the shape of a wind compensator placed sideways to the direction of flight immediately above the projectile outlet orifice. This was applied, for example, to the rotatable B-Stand DL 131/10 weapon position.

The exhaust ports for the empty cartridges in the fuselage sides and cockpit floor were also covered by an aerodynamic fairing. This covering is clearly visible on the C-Stand. In the Ju 188, belt-fed ammunition was used exclusively via metre-long flexible conveyors or circuits, the spent cartridges being ejected through shafts. The gunner therefore had only minimal contact with the exchange of the

Opposite page: **The tables give details of weapons and gunsights of selected Ju 188 series models.**

Below: **Ju 188 Zerstörer mock-up with the expanded nose A-Stand.**

The Ju 188 Level- and Dive-bomber, 1943

Armament	Gun-mount Type	Weapon or Item	No of Rounds	Manufacturer
1. A-Stand	L 151/3	–	–	Ikaria
	–	1 x MG 151/20	200, belt-fed	Mauser
2. B1-Stand	LLG 131	–	–	Ikaria
	–	1 x MG 131	500, belt-fed	Rh.-Borsig
3. B2-Stand	HD 151/2	–	–	LAB
	–	1 x MG 151/20	450, belt-fed	Mauser
4. C-Stand	WL 81Z	–	–	LAB
	–	1 x MG 81Z	1000 ea. belt-fed	Mauser
5. H-Stand (manned)	HL 131Z	–	–	Ikaria
	–	2 x MG 131	600 ea. belt-fed	Rh.-Borsig
6. A-Stand gunsight for fixed firing	Revi C 12C	–	Zeiss-Jena	

Ju 188E Level- and Dive-bomber, 1943 (weapon attachments)

1. Fuselage weapon mounts
a) Forward weapons bay	2 rails, 4 Schloss 50/X (fuselage side walls)	MVN
Bombload: 18 x 50kg = 900kg	2 rails, 5 Schloss 50/X (fuselage centreline)	MVN
b) Rear weapons bay	2 rails, 4 Schloss 50/X (fuselage side walls)	MVN
Bombload: 10 x 50kg = 500kg	1 frame, 2 Schloss 50/X (fuselage centreline)	MVN

2. Wing weapon mounts (identical left & right)
a) Load Type I	Support/ with Schloss 500/1000	(Bombload: max 1,800kg)	Junkers/MWN
b) Load Type II	Support: ETC 500/IXSAM	(Bombload: max 500kg)	
c) Load Type III	Support: ETC 500/IXSAM	(Bombload: max 500kg)	

3. Dive-bombing sight   BZA bombsight   Zeiss-Ikon

4. Level-attack bombsight   Lotfe 7C (Zeiss-Jena) or BZG 2 (Zeiss-Ikon)

Ju 188G-3 with Torpedo-Rüstsatz, 1944/45

Armament	Gun-mount Type	Weapon or Item	No of Rounds	Manufacturer
1. A-Stand	L 151/3	–	–	Ikaria
	–	1 x MG 151/20	200, belt-fed	Mauser
2. B1-Stand	LLG 131E	–	–	Ikaria
	–	1 x MG 131	500, belt-fed	Rh.-Borsig
3. B2-Stand	HD 151/2	–	–	LAB
	–	1 x MG 151/20	450, belt-fed	Mauser
4. C-Stand	WL 81Z	–	–	LAB
	–	1 x MG 81Z	1000 ea. belt-fed	Mauser
5. H-Stand (manned)	RL 131Z	–	–	Ikaria
	–	2 x MG 131	–	Rh.-Borsig
6. Gunsight	–	Revi C 12C	–	Zeiss-Jena
7. Torpedo release gear:				
Supports:	2 PVC 1006B on LS I	–	–	MVN
Torpedoes:	–	2 x LT F5 or F5w	–	–
8. Torpedo sighting gear:	Torpedokommandogerät ToKG			LGW

Ju 188J Night-fighter, 1944 Project

Armament	Gun-mount Type	Weapon or Item	No of Rounds	Manufacturer
1. A-Stand*	Junkers	2 x MG 151	200 ea. belt-fed	Mauser
2. B-Stand	2 x LL-X 81VE	–	–	Ikaria
	–	2 x MG 81	750 ea. belt-fed	Mauser
3. Oblique upward	StL 151/7	–	–	LAB
	–	1 x MG 151/20	200 ea. belt-fed	Mauser
4. Fixed weapons	StL 151/7	–	–	LAB
	–	3 x MG 151/20	–	Mauser
5. Gunsight for forward firing	–	Revi 16B	–	Zeiss-Jena
6. Gunsight for upward firing	–	Revi 16B	–	Zeiss-Jena

*Traversable for horizontal and upward firing.

ammunition feed canisters. The movement of the long ammunition belts was facilitated by auxiliary motor-driven feedbelts. For centre of gravity reasons, the majority of the ammunition was housed in the middle of the fuselage and only a small proportion, mainly in storage containers, was housed directly in the MG-Stand. The drives for the weapons system and centring the weapons took place either electrically or hydraulically, so that the gunner was able to concentrate fully on his task.

At the end of 1943, trials with new types of weapons were carried out with a Ju 188 at the RLM E-Stelle Tarnewitz in the Bay of Wismar. Secret trials had begun there as early as 1937 for equipping aircraft with rocket-driven projectiles. The Rheinmetall-Borsig firm in Berlin-Tegel had developed the cylindrical RZ 65 projectile of 73mm (2.87in) calibre, and armed with this weapon a Ju 188 was used in a series of tests to assess its suitability when directed against railway wagons and light seaborne targets. But despite a satisfactory number of hits, mainly achieved due to its fragmentation effects, this type of weapon was not employed in service use. Testing of other types of rocket-powered missiles, some partly with remote guidance, was also conducted but did not pass the prototype test stage.

Despite the Ju 188's combat capabilities, it displayed a general weakness in terms of defensive armament during its operational deployment in differing combat theatres. As with all models of the Ju 88-series, a blind angle on the Ju 188 directly behind the empennage was not covered by its range of fire. It was hoped to overcome this by means of a remote-controlled FA 15 tail barbette equipped with two superimposed 13mm MG 131 machine-guns, but the construction of a mock-up and the corresponding weapon stand developed at the Junkers parent plant in Dessau failed to solve the problem. As a result of RLM pressure for a solution, a manned tail-gun position was evolved, the proposal being tested with the aid of various mock-up designs. After successfully solving the ergonomic problems of the tail gunner's safety in the event of the aircraft suffering damage due to enemy action or otherwise, a series of static and flight tests using a Ju 88A-4 as a flying test-bed were begun, together with parallel-running wind-tunnel tests. Practical flight-testing, however, did not proceed satisfactorily, so the manned tail-gun stand did not enter operational service on the Ju 188. As an alternative to the rearward field of fire restricted by the presence of the tail surfaces behind the B1-Stand, a design improvement was made whereby the antenna mast could be retracted during air combat by means of an electrically operated telescopic guide rail. However, an improvement to the radius of fire was primarily brought about as a result of a modified empennage design on the Ju 188.

During the course of the war, weapons technology had developed to such a point where the tail gunner merely had the task of aligning and firing his weapons. He had become the functional component of a logistically designed and highly technological war machine in which the chief aim was to destroy the enemy even more speedily.

The Ju 188 was therefore the elite member, the 'Adonis', of the Ju 88 family of aircraft. From the design and technological aspect, it represented the almost ideal aerodynamic configuration according to the technical know-how of its time, and presented a strikingly aesthetic image which endures even today. It was one of the finest propeller-driven aircraft of World War Two, which through its weaponry became an ambassador of death and destruction. In mythology, in spite of his weapons, the handsome Adonis was killed by a wild boar during a hunt. Ironically, however, the majority of the Ju 188s were not destroyed in battle but on the ground due to lack of fuel.

The automatic cartridge feed and ejection for all Ju 188 weapons, as seen here for the twin MG 81Z.

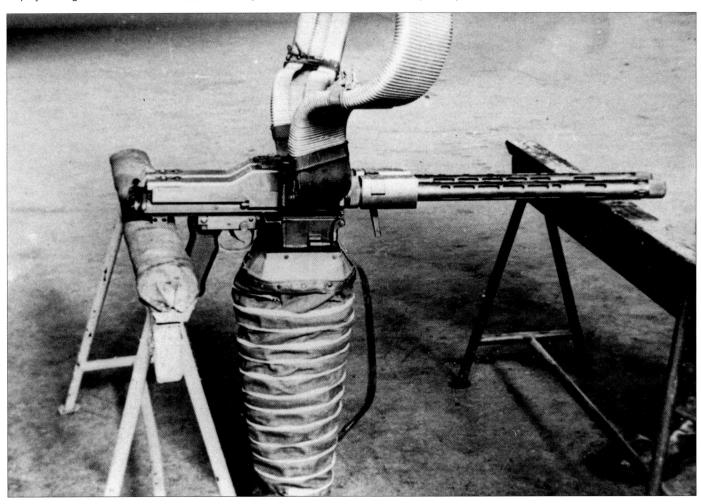

Ju 188E-2 sectional view of the B2-Stand.

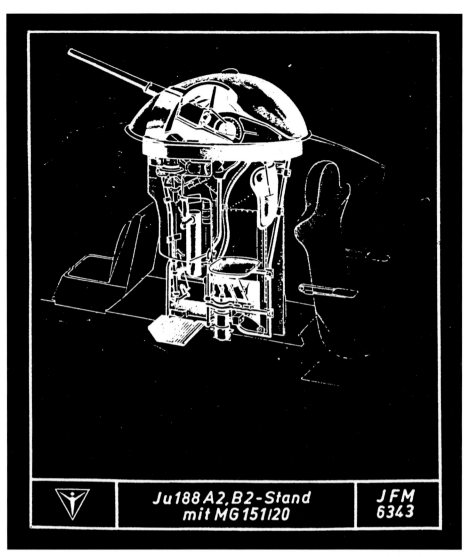

Ju 188 A2, B2-Stand
mit MG 151/20

JFM
6343

Twin underwing bomb suspension points on the Ju 188.

H-Stand (tail gunner's position) on the Ju 188G-0.

This prototype tail-gun layout did not enter series production.

Photographs on the opposite page:

Top: **Ju 188A-2 dorsal weapons: (upper) B1-Stand and (lower) B2-Stand.**

Bottom: **The Ju 88 V27 (D-AWLN) B1- and B2-Stands in comparison.**

Above: **Experimental model of the planned remote-control H-Stand in the Ju 188G-series.**

Left: **View of the tail gunner's seat, harness and controls.**

Below: **Remote-controlled MG 131 tail gun in the Ju 188G-1.**

Photograph on the opposite page:

The heavy bombing raids by the 8th USAAF on 30th May, 20th July and 16th August 1944 on the JFM at Dessau also delayed further development of the Ju 188 and successor models.

A-54898 A.C.

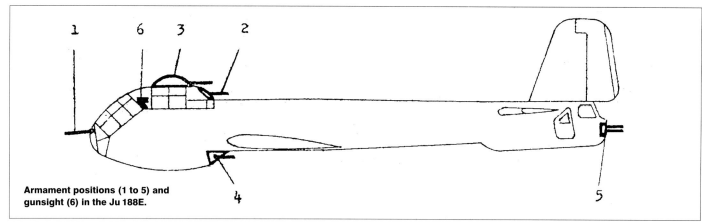

Armament positions (1 to 5) and gunsight (6) in the Ju 188E.

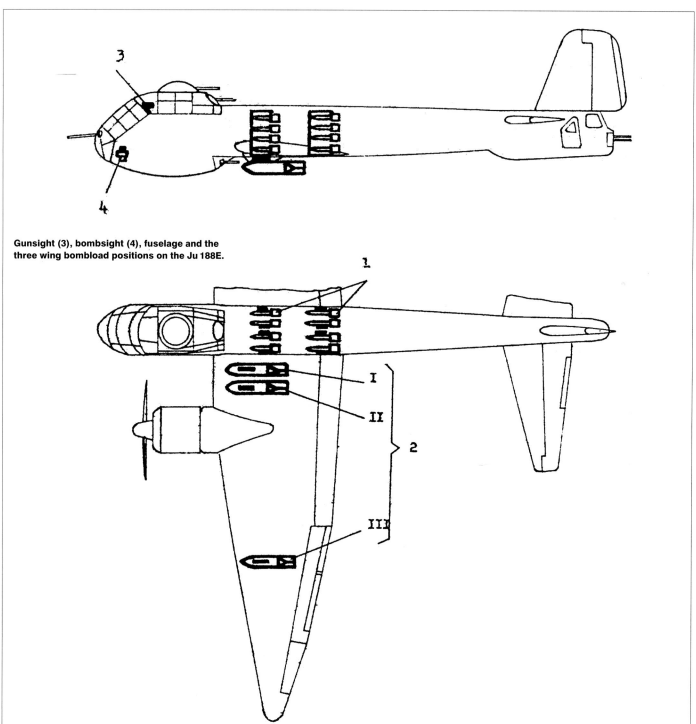

Gunsight (3), bombsight (4), fuselage and the three wing bombload positions on the Ju 188E.

Ju188G-3 armament, torpedo and weapon-sight positions.

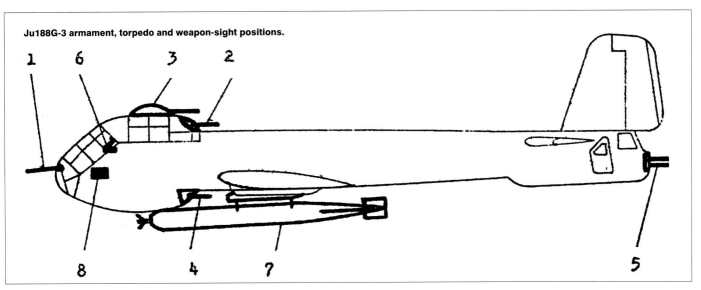

Proposed armament for the Ju 188J project.

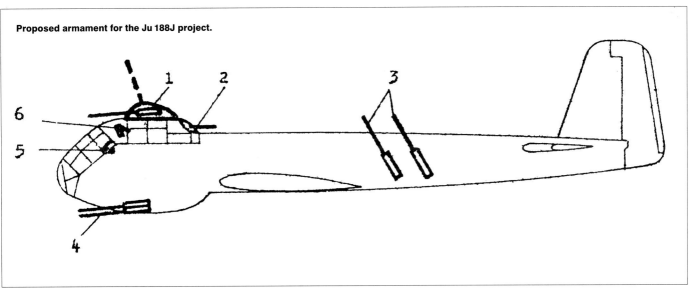

Below: **A captured Ju 188D-2 seen here in RAF markings (Air Min 113). After the war, it was thoroughly examined at the Royal Aircraft Establishment (RAE) at Farnborough, flight-tested and then scrapped.**

Original Junkers illustration of the Ju 188 two-tone camouflage pattern.

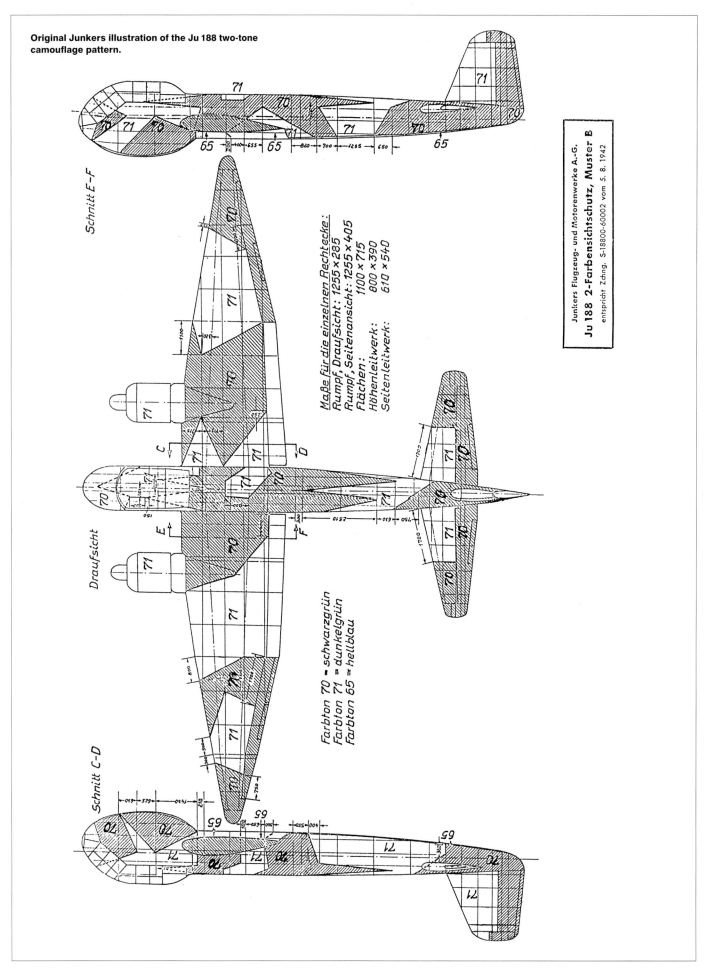

Schnitt E–F

Schnitt C–D

Draufsicht

Junkers Flugzeug- und Motorenwerke A.-G.
Ju 188 2-Farbensichtschutz, Muster B
entspricht Zchng. S-18800-60002 vom 5. 8. 1942

Maße für die einzelnen Rechtecke:
Rumpf, Draufsicht: 1255 × 285
Rumpf, Seitenansicht: 1255 × 405
Flächen: 1100 × 715
Höhenleitwerk: 800 × 390
Seitenleitwerk: 610 × 540

Farbton 70 = schwarzgrün
Farbton 71 = dunkelgrün
Farbton 65 = hellblau

External design differences, colours and markings of the
Ju 88D-1, Ju 188F-1 and Ju 388L-1 respectively.

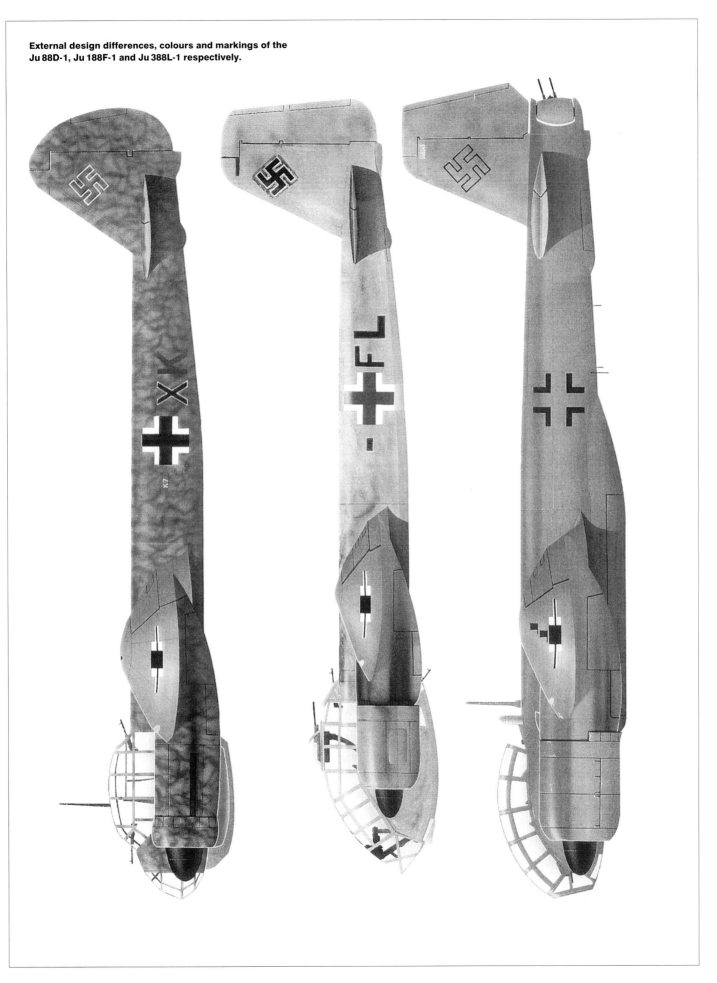

Chapter Seven

The Ju 188 in Scale

Hints for the Modeller

Today, no original example of the Ju 188 exists. None survived the war, and no parts or larger assembly components of the aircraft are available in any aviation and technology museum. Comparisons therefore have to be based exclusively on surviving technical documents. A considerable aid, however, is the still extant and preserved Ju 388L-1 in storage for the National Air & Space Museum in Silver Hill, Maryland, USA. The Americans found this intact example on 19th April 1945 in the Junkers plant in Merseburg. For an interim period this was housed in two large aircraft hangars at the Luftwaffe airbase which was used as a dispersal centre. Except for a few alterations to the instrumentation carried out by the Americans during the course of flight tests, it incorporates the air-conditioned pressurised cockpit and complete internal equipment and fittings of the Ju 188 module. The shape of the lowered cockpit trough, however, conforms to that of the Ju 388. A more detailed inspection of the fuselage reveals identification plates on some of the component parts whose numbers trace their source to the Ju 188, and hints at the interchangeability of certain component groups striven for by Junkers within the Ju 88 'family'.

The development cycle is thus completed. For those who are interested in specific details, it is almost certain that more will be discovered in this respect in the future. Mention should also be made here of the historic 1/25th scale model of the Ju 188 completed in 1943, accurate to the finest detail, made out of highly polished silver plate in the modelling workshop within the experimental construction department of the JFM in Dessau. It was made for display purposes by the then 70-year-old sheet-metal worker Karl Hampusch. At least two such models are known to have been completed and were in the possession of Dr. Eberhard von Brauchitsch, a member of the JFM Board of Directors, and Generalluftzeugmeister Erhard Milch of the RLM. One of these models reappeared in 1992 in a Hamburg fine art dealer's showroom, and because of its precise detail is illustrated here.

In the specialist trade, two kits of the Ju 188 are currently offered in two different scales. Because of their variable profiling possibilities as models, they represent an excellent reduced-size copy of the original. Naturally, a considerable degree of expertise is required in order to capture the exact detailing of the particular variant – a challenge every modeller will happily accept. Much of the pleasure of working on it comes from observing and comparing details and adding the finishing touches to the most delicate of hand-finished details. There is much for the modelmaker to note and compare in this book to enable him to create each variant accurately.

At this point I must thank Damian Güttner of the Plastic Modelmakers Club, Bodensee e.V. (Lake Constance Registered Association) as well as Thomas Erfurth and Martin Kuras of the Hugo Junkers Modelling Association in Dessau, who very kindly made available models and photographs respectively for this publication.

But what use is the finest model when its history is not known? It has therefore been an important aim of this book to present the many aspects of the history of the aircraft and its development within the context of that time. It is only in this way that one can gain a greater knowledge of the Ju 188 through an appreciation of its fascinating technology and its multifaceted adaptability.

Two views of the historic all-metal 1/25th scale model of the 1943-built Ju 188 with open bomb compartments.

Two views of a 1/48th scale Ju 188 plastic model, a Dragon kit conversion by Damian Güttner.

Two views of a 1/72nd scale Matchbox model by Thomas Erfurth.

Two more views of the 1/72nd scale Matchbox model by Thomas Erfurth.

Two views of a 1/72nd scale Matchbox model of the Ju 188 by Thomas Erfurth.

A top view of a 1/72nd scale Matchbox model of the Ju 188 by Martin Kuras.

JAGDWAFFE SERIES VOLUME ONE

Volume 1, Section 1
Birth of Luftwaffe Fighter Force
Softback , 303 x 226 mm, 96 pages
c250 photos. 0 952686 75 9 **£12.95**

Volume 1, Section 2
The Spanish Civil War
Softback , 303 x 226 mm, 96 pages
c250 photos. 0 952686 76 7 **£12.95**

Volume 1, Section 3
Blitzkrieg & Sitzkrieg 1939-40
Softback , 303 x 226 mm, 96 pages
c250 photos. 0 952686 77 5 **£12.95**

Volume 1, Section 4
Attack in the West 1940
Softback, 303 x 226 mm, 96 pages
c250 photos. 0 952686 78 3 **£12.95**

JAGDWAFFE SERIES VOLUME TWO

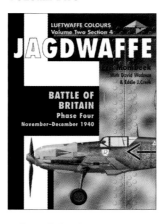

Volume 2, Section 1
BoB Phase 1: June-July 1940
Softback, 303 x 226 mm, 96 pages
c250 photos. 1 903223 05 9 **£14.95**

Volume 2, Section 2
BoB Phase 2: Aug-Sept 1940
Softback, 303 x 226 mm, 96 pages
c250 photos. 1 903223 06 7 **£14.95**

Volume 2, Section 3
BoB Phase 3: Sept-Oct 1940
Softback, 303 x 226 mm, 96 pages
c250 photos. 1 903223 07 5 **£14.95**

Volume 2, Section 4
BoB Phase 4: Oct-Dec 1940
Softback, 303 x 226 mm, 96 pages
c250 photos. 1 903223 08 3 **£14.95**

JAGDWAFFE SERIES VOLUME THREE

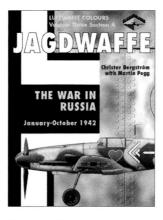

Volume 3, Section 1
Strike in the Balkans: April-May 1941
Softback , 303 x 226 mm, 96 pages
c250 photos. 1 903223 20 2 **£14.95**

Volume 3, Section 2
Barbarossa: Invasion of Russia April-
May 1941. Sbk, 303 x 226 mm, 96pp
c250 photos. 1 903223 21 0 **£14.95**

Volume 3, Section 3
War over the Desert: N Africa June 1940
to June 1942. Sbk, 303 x 226 mm, 96pp,
c250 photos. 1 903223 22 9 **£14.95**

Volume 3, Section 4
The War in Russia: Jan-Oct 1942
Softback, 303 x 226 mm, 96 pages
c250 photos. 1 903223 16 4 **£14.95**

JAGDWAFFE VOLUME 4/1
Holding the West: Jun 1941-Aug 1943

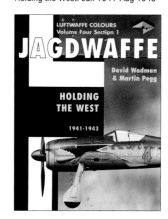

After the Battle of Britain, RAF Fighter
Command went on the offensive, taking
the fight for air superiority to the coast
of Europe. With the bulk of Luftwaffe
units transferred to Russia or the Middle
East, only two were left to defend
France and the occupied countries.
Despite its numerical advantage the
RAF was unable to achieve its aims and
suffered heavy losses. This is the story
of the German fighter force, holding all
the advantages of fighting over its own
territory, in its defensive and offensive
operations against growing Allied might.

Sbk, 303 x 226 mm, 96pp 17 colour
and 229 b/w photos, 27 colour profiles.
1 903223 34 2 **£14.95**

GERMAN SECRET FLIGHT TEST CENTRES TO 1945

H Beauvais, K Kössler, M Mayer
and C Regel

A group of German authors, some of
whom were involved at the time have
brought together a history and overview
of the establishment and activities of
government flight-test centres in
Germany from its resumption in the
1920s until the end of the Second
World War. Major locations included
are the research facilities at
Johannisthal, Lipetsk, Rechlin,
Travemünde, Tarnewitz and
Peenemünde-West.

Hardback, 282 x 213mm, 248 pages
270 b/w photos, sketches, 8pp of col
1 85780 127 X **£35.00**

HELICOPTERS OF THE THIRD REICH

S Coates with J C Carbonel

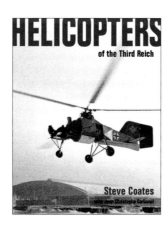

By the end of the Second World War,
the Germans were, despite minimal
funding and bitter inter-service rivalries,
technologically ahead of their American
counterparts in the development of
rotating-wing aircraft. This book is the
first comprehensive account of the
development of auto-gyros and
helicopters in Germany during 1930 to
1945 and sheds light on an unjustly
neglected area of considerable
aeronautical achievement.

Hardback, 303 x 226 mm, 224 pages,
470 b/w and colour photos, plus dwgs
1 903223 24 5 **£35.00**

MESSERSCHMITT Me 163 VOLUME ONE

S Ransom & Hans-Hermann Cammann

The first of two volumes on the legendary
rocket-powered interceptor. The
authors have unearthed incredible new
documentary material and previously
unpublished photos and have received
co-operation from many former pilots.

Focuses on the pre-war design and
development of tailless aircraft as well
the type's deployment by Erprobungs-
kommando 16. There is also a detailed
study of production and an introduction
to its operational use by JG 400.

Hardback, 303 x 226 mm, 224 pages,
200 photos, colour artworks and dwgs
1 903223 12 1 **£35.00**

MESSERSCHMITT Me262

J Richard Smith & Eddie Creek

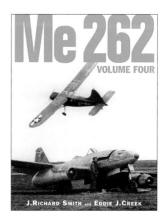

Volume One (revised reprint)
Hbk, 303 x 226 mm, 224pp ,c300 b/w,
colour photos, colour artworks, dwgs
1 903223 10 5 **£35.00**

Volume Two (out of stock)
Reprint under consideration

Volume Three
Hbk, 303 x 226 mm, 228pp ,c300 b/w,
colour photos, colour artworks, dwgs
1 903223 00 8 **£35.00**

Volume Four
Hbk, 303 x 226 mm, 228pp, c350 b/w,
colour photos, colour artworks, dwgs
1 903223 04 0 **£35.00**

Select Bibliography

Der befohlene Untergang – Das Schicksal der Deutschen Luftwaffe (The Ordered Demise – The Fate of the German Luftwaffe): W Berthold; Klagenfurt/Munich, 1998.

Geheimprojekt Mittelbau (Secret Project 'Central Works'): M Bornemann: Bonn, 1994

Aufklärer und Aufklärungsflugzeuge der Deutschen Luftwaffe (Observation and Reconnaissance Aircraft of the German Air Force) 1935-1945: Bradley/Ketley/Wadman; Bonn, 1999

Junkers-Flugzeuge (Junkers Aircraft) 1933-1945: Bukowsky/Griehl; Friedberg, 1991

Kampfflugzeuge und Aufklärer (Bombers and Reconnaissance Aircraft): R Cescotti: Koblenz, 1989

Taktische Militärflugzeuge in Deutschland 1925 bis heute (Tactical Military Aircraft in Germany from 1925 till Today): Dressel/Griehl; Friedberg, 1992

Der Luftkrieg (The Air War): G W Feuchter; Frankfurt/Bonn, 1964

Flugmotoren und Strahltriebwerke (Piston- and Jet-propulsion Aero-engines): Von Gersdorff/Grassmann/Schubert; Bonn, 1995

Famous Bombers of the Second World War: William Green; London, 1960

Geschichte des Luftkrieges (History of the Air War): O Groehler; Berlin, 1981

Anhalt im Lufkrieg (Anhalt during the War): O Groehler; Dessau, 1993

Die geheimen Konferenzen des Generalluftzeugmeisters (The GL Secret Conferences): G Hentschel; Koblenz, 1989

Hitlers Strategie – Politik und Kriegführung (Hitler's Strategy – Politics and War Leadership) 1940-1941: A Hillgruber; Bonn, 1993

Die Tragödie der Deutschen Luftwaffe (The Tragedy of the German Air Force): David Irving; Frankfurt/Berlin, 1970

Kriegstagebuch des Oberkommando der Wehrmacht (The OKW War Diaries) 1940-1945; H A Jacobsen/P E Schramm; 8 Volumes, Munich, 1982

Junkers Flugzeug- und Motorenwerke AG documents:
- Ju 188E-1 und F-1 Baubeschreibung vom 10.01.1943
- Kurz-Baubeschreibung des Bombers Ju 188G-2 vom 14.12.1943
- Ju 188 Flugzeug-Handbuch, Teil 1 to Teil 10 vom 1943
- Ju 188 – Bedienvorschriften, Ausgaben von April und Juli 1943
- JFM Lehrmittel-Vorträge Nr. 25 – Nr.36
- Prüfendberichte zwischen 1942 und 1944
- Versuchsberichte der JFM Kobü-Flugtechnik
- Der Technische Vertrieb, eine Untergruppe des Technischen Buros, Bericht vom 29.04.1944
- Nachlass des Flugzeugkonstrukteurs Ernst Zindel
- Akten im Deutschen Museum München, 1942-45, relating to Ju 188

Die Luftwaffe (The Luftwaffe): Kollektiv; Eltville, 1993

Luftkriegsführung im Zweiten Weltkrieg (Air War Leadership In World War Two): Kollektiv; Herford/Bonn, 1993

Typenhandbuch der Deutschen Luftfahrttechnik (Type-Handbook of German Aviation Technology): B Lange; Koblenz, 1986

Fliegende Front (The Flying Front): W E Von Medem; Berlin, 1942

Ju 188/Ju 388 Part 1: R Michulec; Danzig, 1997

Ju 188/Ju 388 Part 2: R Michulec; Danzig, 1997

Junkers-Patente von 1892-1945: W Miertsch; 7 Volumes, Wildau bei Berlin, 1998 (unpublished documents)

Der Einsatz der Deutschen Luftwaffe Über dem Atlantik und der Nordsee (German Air Force Operations Over the Atlantic and North Sea): S Neitzel; Bonn, 1995

H J Nowarra: Die Deutsche Luftrüstung (The German Air Armament Programme) 1933-1945 Volume 3: S Neitzel; Koblenz, 1993

Die Ju 88 und ihre Folgemuster (The Ju 88 and its Successors): H J Nowarra; Stuttgart, 1987

Junkers-Bilderatlas aller Flugzeugtypen (Junkers Picture Atlas of All Aircraft Types) 1910-1945: G Schmitt; Berlin 1990

Das Junkers-Flugzeugtypenbuch (Type-book of Junkers Aircraft): G Schmitt; Dessau, 1997

Hugo Junkers – Pionier der Luftfahrt – Seine Flugzeuge (Hugo Junkers – Aviation Pioneer – His Aircraft): W Wagner; Bonn, 1996